An Anthropological Guide to the Art and Philosophy of Mirror Gazing

Thinking in the World
Series editors: Jill Bennett and Mary Zournazi

Thinking in the World combines the work of key thinkers to pioneer a new approach to the study of thought. Responding to a pressing need in both academic and wider public contexts to account for thinking as it is experienced in everyday settings, the Reader and Book Series explore our thinking relationship to everything from illness, to built environments, to ecologies, to other forms of life and technology.

Bringing together phenomenology with recent trends in cognitive science and the arts, this unique, field-defining collection illuminates thinking as a practical activity. It interweaves a series of distinctive essays and commentaries into a compelling whole, constituting a new framework and set of resources for analyzing thinking in real-world situations. Rather than simply thinking *about* the world, the authors examine the ways in which we think *in and with* the world in its physical, material and social dimensions. A philosophy of thinking in action, it provides a multifaceted but sustained account of neurobiological experience and its inexorable connection to the world.

Other titles in the series

Thinking in the World, ed. Jill Bennett and Mary Zournazi
Practical Aesthetics, ed. Bernd Herzogenrath (forthcoming)

An Anthropological Guide to the Art and Philosophy of Mirror Gazing

Maria Danae Koukouti &
Lambros Malafouris

BLOOMSBURY ACADEMIC
LONDON • NEW YORK • OXFORD • NEW DELHI • SYDNEY

BLOOMSBURY ACADEMIC
Bloomsbury Publishing Plc
50 Bedford Square, London, WC1B 3DP, UK
1385 Broadway, New York, NY 10018, USA
29 Earlsfort Terrace, Dublin 2, Ireland

First published in Great Britain 2021
This paperback edition published in 2022

Cover design by Charlotte Daniels
Cover images: Deer © awhelin / iStock Mirror © Andrea Borile / EyeEm / Getty Images

A catalogue record for this book is available from the British Library.

Library of Congress Cataloging-in-Publication Data

Names: Koukouti, Maria Danae, author. | Malafouris, Lambros, author.
Title: An anthropological guide to the art and philosophy of mirror gazing / Maria Danae
Koukouti & Lambros Malafouris.
Description: London; New York: Bloomsbury Academic, 2020. |
Series: Thinking in the world | Includes bibliographical references and index. |
Summary: "The ability to look at one's face in the mirror and the ability to find one's self in the
mirror are two quite different things. The former is a natural capacity that humans share with
other animals; the latter is an acquired skill that only humans can master. The craft of mirror-gazing,despite its
relevance to daily life is barely understood. An Anthropological Guide to the Art and Philosophy of Mirror
Gazing provides a metaphysical manual to understand it. The book is written from a cross-disciplinary and
object-based perspective. The role of the mirror as a technology of self-objectification is explored
through various case studies of cultures such as the Buryats of Eastern Mongolia.
By using various anthropological examples, Koukouti and Malafouris survey and reflect on the
structures and experiences of consciousness that underpin the specular image and the different
meanings of the self. By combining metaphor, comparison and estrangement - where what was thought of
as natural is seen as deliberately caused and altered - this book weaves together ethnographic description and
philosophical analysis with empirical examples and experimental studies that allow the reader to
think about the world and their subjectivity a bit differently"– Provided by publisher.
Identifiers: LCCN 2020019592 (print) | LCCN 2020019593 (ebook) | ISBN 9781350135154 (hardback) |
ISBN 9781350135161 (ebook) | ISBN 9781350135178 (epub)
Subjects: LCSH: Self-perception–Case studies. | Self-consciousness (Awareness)–Case studies. |
Classification: LCC BF697.5.S43 K68 2020 (print) |
LCC BF697.5.S43 (ebook) | DDC 155.2–dc23
LC record available at https://lccn.loc.gov/2020019592
LC ebook record available at https://lccn.loc.gov/2020019593

ISBN: HB: 978-1-3501-3515-4
PB: 978-1-3502-0263-4
ePDF: 978-1-3501-3516-1
eBook: 978-1-3501-3517-8

Series: Thinking in the World

Typeset by Integra Software Services Pvt. Ltd.

To find out more about our authors and books visit www.bloomsbury.com
and sign up for our newsletters.

For Odysseus

Contents

Acknowledgements

This book took many years to write. Not least because the connections that defined its final shape were not even remotely visible at the beginning of our endeavour. What we eventually discovered, in the process of writing this book, was very different from what we had originally planned or imagined. On reflection, we have been surprised by the range of perspectives, and the sources of intellectual inspiration (both human and non-human) that have influenced our thinking.

Looking back, we can only be thankful to our editors Liza Thompson, Lucy Russell and Jill Bennet. Many thanks especially to Mary Zournazi for her unfailing support, good advice and immense patience. We have been also very lucky to find ourselves in an environment – the University of Oxford – full of enthusiastic people who have helped shape our thoughts and experiences over the years. We owe a particular debt of gratitude to the following friends and colleagues for reading and commenting on various chapters and passing on some excellent ideas: Miranda Creswell, Rory Carnegie, David Van Oss, Richard Briant and Chris Gosden. Fred Coolidge deserves very special thanks for reading the final draft in its entirety and providing extensive comments and constructive criticism that helped increase the clarity of our arguments. Of course, we are responsible for all remaining errors or inconsistencies. We would like to thank also Katerina Fotopoulou and Carey Jewitt for many and varied conversations on these and other topics. We are also very grateful to Francesco Parisi and the other participants of the conference Mediating Material Engagement in Messina where Maria Danae Koukouti presented a precis of the book. We have benefited greatly also from discussions with Claudio Paolucci.

Many institutions have contributed to the book. A significant part of Lambros Malafouris' work on this book was supported by the John Templeton Foundation and the Keble College Small Research Grant. Also since 2018 our work in Oxford has been funded by the European Research Council (ERC) Consolidator Grant, HANDMADE (No 771997) awarded to Lambros Malafouris. We are immensely grateful to the above Institutions for their support.

Above all else we thank our son Odysseus, who has grown to a young adult over the years during which the book were written, for his love and understanding.

Image and imagination: A prolegomenon

Let's start with something imaginary: a mirror placed in a clearing in the middle of a forest. It stands upwards placed on the ground. The mirror is unframed. The surrounding forest is feral. Suddenly, a deer appears from an opening. It runs for a while, then it stops. It looks back at the edge of the forest, then looks around. It gives a final glance at the trees before turning its gaze towards the middle of the forest where the mirror stands. Can the deer see the mirror? Let's assume that it does. What does the deer see inside the mirror? We can hardly imagine. To find out we must be patient. We must wait for the deer to come closer and look for itself. We watch the deer as it moves hesitantly. It now stands in front of the mirror looking at its own reflection. What can it possibly see or discover? In our eyes, the mirror image of the deer signifies an absence: the absence of the deer's physical body that stands by the mirror, facing it. In the eyes of the deer, however, what for us is an absence may well be a presence: the presence of another deer living behind the mirror. In this imaginary plot, we are all (the deer, us, the mirror, the mirror image, the forest, the middle) caught up in a game of mimesis, of presences and absences, of living bodies and lifeless reflections. Maybe without knowing it, we have anticipated from the start, even hoped, that the deer will fall for the mirror we placed in the middle of the forest. What we didn't expect, imagine or wish for is that this mimetic transaction may well bring about the death of the deer. More often than not, whether the plot is imagined or real, the mirror is a hunter, hiding in the middle of the forest, in between self and other. The strangest, but also interesting, things in human life happen in the 'middle'. Perhaps those in-between happenings can also be understood as relationships between hunters and prey. These are primarily mimetic relationships that involve a participatory logic, that is, a logic that connects. Naturally, hunter and prey relationships embody a killing dialogue that inevitably leads both hunter and prey to self-identification. Captured in the representational distance and capitalist ethos of modern societies, we find it hard to think along those connective lines. We have lost our ability to think in sympathetic terms. We have forgotten the language of traces and trails, and know very little of hunters and prey. Yet, our new forests are full of boundary objects and mimetic devices that if touched in the right way can help us remember and reclaim our lost hunting skills. In this book we set out to follow one of those objects: we know it as the mirror.

1

About mirroring: An introduction

'I' see 'me'

This book started with the imaginary and must turn now to the ordinary. We take that most readers know what it is like to look in the mirror and assume that, under normal conditions, one is able to recognize one's own image in it. Presumably, we know much less about mirror images, their modes of being or the impact they may have on our lives. Nevertheless, we seem confident about the use we can make of this object of 'perpetual fascination' and everyday magic.[1] Indeed, once you get to know it and come to trust its surface, the mirror is a self-explanatory device. It attracts your gaze and performs its mimetic function (what we call 'mirroring'),[2] asking nothing in return. You don't need to know why or how it works, and you don't need to do anything to make it work; it simply does. In fact, it works so well that even other species can use it (if they are offered the chance).

However, as it is often the case with most mimetic creatures, natural or artificial, simplicity is misleading. Mirrors do more than mirroring. More than just presenting our image (a body or a face), they actively influence our experience of selfhood (the consciousness of being that body or that face). This potent capacity of the mirror to act as a powerful device of self-identification will be the main focus of this book. We take the mirror as an opportunity to rethink the question of selfhood. Our stated objective also reveals something of our major assumptions: we all have a self somewhere even if that self is transitional, illusory and incomplete. Self is not a stable entity but a multifaceted process. We take that mirror gazing constitutes such a process or technique of self-becoming. Expressed by way of a single overarching objective, our aim is to provide a comparative anthropological enquiry of what it is to look and find a self in the mirror. We dub this the art of mirror self-identification: it can be conceived as a way of knowing things (*episteme*) as much as a way of doing things (*techné*).

The sceptic may object to these theoretical complications: 'Thanks but last time I looked there was nothing especially difficult or interesting about finding myself in the mirror – especially early in the morning.' It is very hard to think of the mirror as anything other than a piece of reflecting glass. You see, we are used to look at the world in a certain way. But it is exactly that degree of familiarity that costs us its magic and promise. Indeed, what we often fail to realize is that looking at oneself in the mirror and finding oneself in the mirror are two quite different things. One would think that, especially nowadays, living in an environment surrounded by mirroring surfaces of all sorts, and given the time we spend in front of the mirror, humans would be experts in mirror gazing. Nothing is further from the truth. The more used we are to something, the less likely we are to be enchanted or enlightened by it. The art of mirror self-identification, ancient as it may be, is almost becoming obsolete. Not only do we seem incapable of using the mirror as a tool for the self, we also often suffer from various delusional beliefs about what one's reflection in the mirror might be and what it does. As developmental psychologist Philippe Rochat explains, the '[m]irror reflection of the self is paradoxical in the sense that what is seen in the mirror is the self as another person.'[3] Our own face often becomes a stranger; a stranger's face becomes the 'I'.

What can we learn about the self by taking a different, more critical anthropological stance towards the mirror? If the mirror is an active participant in our daily routines of self-identification (not just mimicking but also constructing and dictating personal narratives), what is it that gives the mirror this power or agency? How does it do it?

Trying to answer those questions, one of the main arguments of this book will be that looking at one's face in the mirror and finding one's self in the mirror are two processes related but distinctive, both with profound psychological consequences. The former process, the ability to identify one's own image in a mirror, requires no special effort or training. All it takes is having a mirror and looking at it. At first the untrained eye may be bedazzled with the dissonant spectacle – sometimes terrified by the sight of its mirror image.[4] But soon habit will ease our anxiety, turning illusion into reality. The second process, finding one's self in the mirror, is more complicated: it presupposes knowing how to look in it. The sufferings and the pleasures that come with this process outlast the period of initial exposure. The quest of self-knowledge through the looking-glass is very different from the visual process of identifying a face or a body in the mirror. Finding our self in the mirror is a skill that demands great effort and care. This skill is also of a different order from the so-called mirror self-recognition test discussed in the relevant experiments with small children and non-human animals.[5] Self-recognition in those experiments speaks of the agency of the mirror and exposes the affordances (in Gibson's[6] sense of interactive possibilities) of this mimetic device. Still, to find one's self in the mirror presents us altogether with a different challenge.

From an optics perspective, there is nothing mysterious in the way a polished surface reflects rays of light showing us how we look. The same cannot be argued, however, from an anthropological perspective concerned with the phenomenology (what is it like) and cognitive ecology of mirroring. When unnoticed and unexamined the mirroring is transparent. It is the moment we start thinking about it that it becomes a problem. What does the mirroring do? What is it made of? What happens when 'I' see 'me' inside the mirror? Once we raise those questions, the mirroring is transformed from a mundane experience into a meshwork of socio-political and material considerations about what exactly happens when the human body, or selective parts of that body (in particular the face), becomes the centre of visual attention. Suddenly, the mirror image can no longer be taken for granted; it is now a source of epistemic enchantment and confusion/dissonance.

The mirroring is enchanting because, quite 'un-naturally', it allows the eye to perform a function deemed useless by natural selection, that is, to gaze at one's own face. Our eyes stare at our staring eyes. To look at our face in the mirror is to gaze directly at that part of the human body that we are not supposed to see, even though it is probably the part we associate with human subjectivity more than any other. Perhaps this explains why the mirroring radiates a sense of awkwardness and law-breaking: we are no longer blind to the 'eye' of the 'I'. Even if, as Ronald Barthes[7] rightly observes for the photographic image, the old 'madness' inherited in autoscopy (the experience of seeing one's body in extrapersonal space) has probably, in our times, been forgotten, the momentary illusion, the split between 'I' and 'me' that comes with mirroring, remains still. So, we may also say that the mirroring is confusing because it is an illusion that cannot lie: on the one hand, what we see in the mirror is nothing but a phantom image of our body standing against the background of an impenetrable shiny surface. But on the other hand, as the semiotician Umberto Eco observes, '[o]nce we have acknowledged that what we perceive is a mirror image, we always begin from the principle that the mirror "tells the truth"'.[8]

Contrary to what Eco's semiotic treatment of the mirror appears to recommend, however, one of the central themes of this book will be that mirrors are not to be trusted. Mirroring, like any other form of re-presentation, is never innocent. Unfailingly, the mirror will try to play its usual tricks on us – to enthral us, to mesmerize us.

Fooled by the mirror

Let's try a simple experiment which we borrow from art historian Ernst Gombrich. Next time you happen to look at the fogged-up mirror of your bathroom, circle the outline of your head with your finger.[9] Then come closer and measure the length of the outline you have just produced. Strange, isn't it? Repeat the experiment as many times as you wish from whatever distance. The result will be the same: the length of the outline of your reflected head is actually half the size of your real head. Surprised? If you are, it is because you, like anyone else, share an unexamined and largely automatic conviction: the mirror always speaks the truth; therefore, it presents real-size reflections. Those of you who tried our experiment now know that this conviction is clearly wrong: an illusion.

So what? Surely, one might think, the world of physical phenomena is full of perceptual illusions of one sort or another. True, but there is a darker side in all this, which often passes unattended. Let us explain. There is a paradox: only a few lines above, it was revealed to you for the first time – at least to those of you unfamiliar with Gombrich's experiment – that all your life you have been fooled by the mirror. Still – and this is where the paradox lies – despite the extent of this treachery, none of you felt the slightest concern or worry. Should one worry?

Indeed, why should one care about a mere mirror illusion? It's not that you've seen a ghost or someone else's face in the mirror or that you tried to get inside the mirror to touch the reflected face behind its surface.[10] No, nothing of this radical sort: what you see is simply smaller than you think. No harm is done. Besides, we are rational, so-called sapient creatures and presumably now that the illusion has been revealed our superintelligence can be fooled no more. Right? Let's find out. Turn your glance towards the mirror and look at your face once more: do you see your mirror face as being half the size of your real face? Obviously, the answer is no. How would that be possible? The psychology of perception has an easy reply: one needs only to realize that the mirror is always located halfway between oneself and our own virtual image.[11] Still, the fact that our image is constantly half the physical size independently of how far we are from the mirror is counterintuitive.

We are all willing to accept that things are not always what they seem. But the reason we can accept this undeniable fact light-heartedly is because of our certainty that knowing our illusions we overcome them. We are certain, in other words, that the logical power of our rational thinking is stronger and, in the end, will prevail and protect us. Unfortunately, this is not what's happening. In fact, it is often the other way around. Maybe then, more important than asking why people stubbornly refuse to see the real size of their faces on the mirror's surface is to ask what else do we fail to notice? We propose that this question is quintessentially anthropological (in both the ethnographic and the philosophical sense of the word). And, as it happens with questions of that kind, they usually demand not just to learn but also to unlearn several things we usually take for granted.

Towards a comparative anthropology of mirror gazing

Analytically speaking, this book can be described as a comparative philosophical anthropology of mirror gazing. We call our approach in this book anthropological not because we want to embark on a detailed ethnographic study or provide a comprehensive coverage of the relevant literature on mirrors. Rather, our intent is critical and comparative. We adopt an anthropological approach primarily because we want to disturb and estrange the familiar so that new connections and patterns of juxtaposition may emerge. Technically, we approach mirroring as a visual mode of material engagement.[12] We are interested to explore how the mirror affects human perception, modes of attention and self-transformation. Indeed, the moment we are exposed to our mirror image we become something else. We insist on integrating 'knowing' and 'doing' because this integration is the best recipe for effecting and understanding this self-transformation. This integration of thought and action also provides the primary stuff or ingredients for a good relational ontology.

Recognizably, putting the right ontological ingredients together at the right time is a difficult task. For this to happen, you need a manual. This book can also be seen as a manual, albeit, of an unusual comparative sort. We understand that speaking of a comparative manual may sound as a contradiction in terms. Manuals, like maps, are meant to be unambiguous and universally applicable. The language of instructions might differ, but the process described must be identical. Yet, a distinctive feature of anthropological enquiry can be seen in the way it reveals the constant tension between similarity and difference as it can be observed in various forms of human biosocial becoming.[13] The practice of mirror gazing is not an exception. Mirror self-identification is an acquired skill, something you learn as a child growing up in a particular historical situation. This is why we propose that the art of mirror gazing involves a great deal of unlearning. Take for instance our shared conviction that the mirror is a solid reflective surface – rather than a forward extension of space. This conviction demands and predisposes us to look 'at' the mirror rather than 'through' it. In our world there is nothing to grab and reach for other than the mirror's cool surface. But what would happen if we were instead to look 'through' the mirror as if it was transparent? Taking such a step requires a perspectival understanding of the world, which allows for ontological multiplicity. That is, the possibility that there is more than a single reality to see inside the mirror, more than one world to navigate, more than a single story to tell. Talk about ontologies is increasingly fashionable among philosophers and anthropologists these days. We will not take issue with the theoretical discussions and debates surrounding 'new materialisms'[14] and 'ontological turn'.[15] Rather, we use the term 'ontology' in a very basic sense, denoting a quintessential form of comparative anthropological enquiry that aims to expose, adding resistance and friction, the reality (what it is that matters) of certain transparent phenomena that may otherwise pass unnoticed or be mischaracterized as elusive or merely imaginary. We are interested to understand *how the mirror matters*[16] and to illustrate some of the multiple ways by which the mirror *comes to matter*. The task is more difficult than what it might seem: as we will see in the following chapters, the mirror will prove to be a profoundly unsettling and unstable piece of vital materiality.[17]

Patterns that connect

Tackling this ontological pluralism of looking in the mirror, this book will set out a creative juxtaposition of stories about the life of the mirror, that is, stories of mirroring and mirror gazing. We take inspiration about how to build our stories from Gregory Bateson's thesis of connectedness. In this context, a 'story' is defined as a 'little knot or complex of that species of connectedness which we call relevance', and following Bateson we will assume 'that any A is relevant to any B if both A and B are parts or components of the same "story"'.[18] Tim Ingold is another anthropologist who used the metaphor of the knot to describe the creative forces of life.[19] The stories we compile in the following chapters aim at providing exactly such a 'pattern that connects',[20] not in the linear sense of causality, but in the sense described by Gilles Deleuze and Félix Guattari as rhizomatic.[21] Rhizomatic connections, like grabgrass, are growing in all directions, with no beginnings and endings. Our stories of mirror gazing are a species of process ontology, they live in the 'middle'. In that sense, they do not serve a taxonomic or classificatory function; rather, the aim is to highlight possible patterns or pathways of connectivity. As Tim Ingold points out, '*stories always, and inevitably, draw together what classifications split apart*'.[22]

To assemble and narrate stories of mirroring in a manner that respects and highlights their ontological proximity and multiplicity is no doubt a difficult task that demands delicate use of metaphor, comparison and estrangement. Metaphor will allow us to conceptualize the unfamiliar through the familiar. Comparison will permit us to re-conceptualize two familiar things in the light of each other. Estrangement will be used to turn the familiar into unfamiliar, and then to resituate the unfamiliar at the very heart of our ordinary habitual life.

In this book, the metaphor that perhaps best exemplifies the above is that of the mirror as trap: we think of mirroring on a par with hunting. The mimetic exchange assumes the relation between hunter and prey. This metaphor, more than just being a 'metaphor', takes us literally into the realm of the non-human, exemplified in this book in the image of a deer. The deer has been invited to walk freely through the pages of our book. It has already made a brief and shy appearance at the very beginning, looking inside the frameless mirror we set for it in the middle of a forest. It returns again many times in different contexts, teaching us all we need to know about hunting. The deer allows us to confront the gaze of the prey. Mirroring is the essence of this confrontation. By mirroring the deer you become the deer. The hunter is turned into prey; the prey becomes the hunter. Highlighting this transformation allows us to reclaim the lost connection between animal and human gaze in the face of victimization. The borders between self and other blur as we finally adopt the animal's gaze. We turn our gaze back at the mirror, but now we have blood on our hands.

Book synopsis

This book is not a history of the mirror as a thing. It is not an ethnography 'of' mirror-things either. Rather, it is an anthropological experiment in comparative *thinging*[23]. That is, we adopt an anthropological stance and use it to expose some hidden aspects of our everyday thinking with, through and about things – specifically, mirror-things. This emphasis on mirroring as *thinging* is crucial for the stories we plan to narrate. The main reason is the following: whereas any language can be used to obscure the inadequacy of its concepts and categories, *thinging* does exactly the opposite: it leaves us conceptually exposed, anxious and insecure.

Important to note also is that although approaching our subject matter we have adopted a critical anthropological stance, we have also avoided to prioritize one disciplinary perspective over the others. Instead, we have sought to represent and discuss those aspects of mirror gazing that we felt have cross-cultural and comparative value in our attempt to expose some hidden dimensions of mirror gazing. Some of the topics we touch upon in the different chapters, deliberately fragmented, have a long tradition of independent scholarship that would have been impossible to summarize. We choose instead to focus on a small number of works that influenced our thinking and helped in the weaving of our argument combining ethnography, philosophy and storytelling, knowing that some readers will be disappointed to see that important works may receive only passing mention or even none at all.

The first two chapters aim to explore the enigmatic, passionate, sometimes even obsessive, relationship with our mirrored-self. In Chapter 2 we ask what exactly is the mirroring? How does it claim our attention? What about it is unique when compared with other media of self-presentation and re-presentation? We try to address those questions comparing self-mirroring to other traditional forms of self-imaging and examining its distinctive qualities of movement and mimicry. A common fallacy about mirrors is to think that they simply hang on the wall.

In Chapter 3 we argue that there is no such thing as a free-standing mirror. Mirrors, we argue, are by definition hand-held objects: our social and historical situation holds the mirror and determines the angle and intensity of light and reflection. As many people know from experience, mirror gazing can turn into a diminishing, abusing affair. This chapter sets out to explore the dark side of the mirror. The punitive mirror gaze of a body fragmented and commodified against the magnifying distorted glass of consumerism and mass propaganda. Can we escape this parody of looking that the advertising industry promotes and imposes on our self-image – always content, forever youthful and eternally energetic? We propose an act of resistance.

In Chapters 4 and 5 we delve into the realm of imagination as expressed in literature, art and popular culture around the world, seeking to reveal some underlying patterns in the human experience and representation of staring into the looking-glass. How do mirrors 'reflect' our imagination? What is it about mirrors that make people everywhere to attribute, almost instinctively, dangerous qualities to them? We propose there is more to the literary mirror than mere imaginings. We follow Alice in her famous journey through the looking-glass to discover a universe of vital materialism and perspectival qualities: from thinking chess pieces and flowers to talking animals and things, the world is inhabited by different persons, human and non-human, all of whom seem to have sentience and agency, as well as a distinctive perspective for connecting to each other and for making sense of the world. What we dare is a bridge – a connective line between fantasy and the enthralling multiplicity of human existence. We do so in order to inhabit as many realities as possible: to step through the looking-glass ourselves. The mirror facilitates us to walk that line by becoming misty and transparent: a mirror one can walk through. What happens when a 'fictional' and a 'real' world mirror each other?

Away from fantasy and into the magic of the real, Chapter 6 is dedicated to the mirrors of Mongolia, a place where, surprisingly, the mirror's purpose is not to be looked at. To the Buryat of Eastern Mongolia mirrors are not just uncanny: they absorb things. Mongolian household mirrors are depositories of past events (like quarrels or a death in the family), which might later leak into the future with grim consequences. That is why mirrors often remain concealed and young children are prohibited to look in them. Drawing on the work of anthropologist Caroline Humphrey,[24] we focus on a special object, the shamanic mirror, the '*toli*': a magical vessel of the dead, a light flashing weapon and a living thing with a will of its own. The shamanic mirror has the ability to move and affect lives, to bring madness, to destroy or reveal psychic energy. How is that possible? We approach the shamanic mirror with care and gaze to its other side where important lessons about what a mirror image is and does can be learned.

This brings us to the last two chapters where the art or skill of mirror self-identification is fully exposed. In Chapter 7 we ask the reader to think of the mirror as a hunting weapon, more specifically, a trap of a rather peculiar perspectival sort. Traps are usually designed to catch particular animals. The more specialized the trap, the more effective it is.[25] The same applies to the mirror. What kind of creatures then a mirror-trap is designed to catch? We suggest that mirror-traps are especially effective with creatures of the self-conscious kind. Every trap signifies a basic need. In the case of the mirror the need is not for food but for self-knowledge. So, how can we tell hunter from prey? To answer that and to better explain the idea of the mirror as trap we follow the Siberian Yukaghirs.[26] They teach us the art of transformative mimicry. We watch them as they disguise themselves to mirror their prey, wear their fur, mimic their moves and become the animals' mirror image. It is a game of sexual seduction. Extending further our hunting metaphor and the idea of the mirror as trap, in the final chapter of the book (Chapter 8) we abandon the gaze of the prey and adopt the gaze of the hunter. We discuss when and how the mirror hurts and come to recognize a 'phantom pain': that of the absent and perfect mirroring we fail to find in the looking-glass. It becomes apparent that, chasing an imaginary and ideal mirrored-self, we surrender the ownership of our bodies. We become, in our minds, amputees. We succumb, as victims, to a narrative of blame. Can we reclaim the ownership of our body? Can we balance the need of owning our body and lives with the constant demand to circulate self-images? We end our journey, perhaps unexpectedly, in psychopathology. The mirror, apart from inflicting pain, can also have a therapeutic effect. Is there a healing mirror? It all depends on how you look at it. The gaze of the hunter is an invitation to see the mirror's enchantment and not just its glass: to find oneself in the mirror but also in the mirror's depths.

Part One

Dis-enchantment

The image thief – a profound madness

Inside the mirror

What's in the mirror? Rarely, if ever, we ask that question. Our mirrored reflection is taken for granted. That's hardly surprising, considering how easily we can all obtain one. We have overcome any initial fear, and we have forgotten the anxiety and perceptual ambiguity we had to suffer, as young children, before we finally succeeded to recognize our self in the mirror for the first time. As adults, although we continue to spend an enormous amount of time looking at the mirror, we rarely bother to think or learn anything from it. As a result, the true enormity of the phenomenological and semiotic challenges that mirroring embodies escapes us. Our gaze stops at the mirror's surface. Implicitly, we also assume that mirror gazing and the various questions of self-imaging that it raises are easily accountable, by means of basic science; no need to ponder on what it is like to see yourself in the mirror. Few of us know what this exact scientific account of mirroring might be, but we trust that there is one, and that it is well understood. If we don't know exactly how and why the mirror works is not because we cannot find the answer to those questions; rather, it is because we do not need to know the answers. The mirror is doing its work regardless. All we need to understand the workings of the mirror is a period of habituation: the opportunity to spend some time with the looking-glass and to learn about its properties by actually engaging with it.

This kind of habituation, and the education of perception that comes with it, is common experience for the modern person. It is not an experience peculiar to mirror gazing but a broader feature of our engagement with all kind of images and forms of imaging. The disenchantment of imaging that characterizes our modern ecology of seeing is a relatively recent phenomenon in human history. As with any other historical synergy of mind and matter (enchanting or disenchanting), it brings about a peculiar set of constraints for looking at and making sense of the world. In the case of mirroring there are two important constraints at work: first, a subject–object separation that reiterates a false dilemma between reality and appearance, and second, a sense of control of the subject over the object that reiterates an illusion of agency. A mirror cannot mirror anything before a subject is able and willing to identify its reflection, or the reflection of some other object, in it. There can be no mirror image in the absence of a perceiving subject. Yet, a peculiarity of the mirror is that the subject gazing at the mirror and the object inside the mirror are one. This semiotic conflation, for as long as it lasts, blurs, if not cancels entirely, the distance between subject and object and creates a vacuum of agency that needs to be filled.

We have learned to think of ourselves as agents who have mastery and control over their mirror image. In reality, things tend to be more complicated than that. This should come as no surprise. We have never been 'the masters of our images, but rather in a sense at their mercy', as the historian of art Hans Belting points out.[1] This basic premise, namely, that 'it is in fact the images that are in control' we believe applies also in the case of the mirror image. How can this be? How can it be that a mirror image that appears leading the life of a shadow can ever exert any kind of control on us? To answer that question, we need to understand better the cognitive life of the mirror image,[2] that is, we need to understand what are the distinctive qualities of mirroring as a form of self-imaging. This would be the major aim of this chapter.

Images that do not travel

Where should we start to examine what kind of image dwells inside the mirror? The question becomes acute once we identify with the help of Umberto Eco one of its peculiar characteristics: 'As long as I look at it, it gives me back my facial features, but if I mailed a mirror which I have long looked at to my beloved, so that she may remember my looks, she could not see me (and would instead see herself)'[3] (Eco 1984, 211). It is with this peculiarity of mirroring that we start. Mirror images do not travel; only mirrors do. This does not mean that mirror images stay still. Quite the contrary, they move in perfect temporal contingency with our own bodily movements. As long as we stay in front of the looking-glass, the mirroring stays with us. The moment we move away from the mirror the mirroring disappears. Paradoxically, in spite of all the movement, our mirrored body eventually vanishes without leaving any visible trace on the mirror's surface. No trace, no memory. Did you ever remember a mirroring? We remember photographs, portraits, videos, even images we saw in our dreams, but we don't seem to recall any specific encounters with our specular image. The mirror image is slippery; it does not attach itself to memory.

The mirror image has no memory; it is not memory either. Why is that? There are many reasons, as we will have the chance to discuss later on and in the chapters to follow. One reason especially relevant to our immediate concerns is the following: unlike the products of other mimetic machines and media – be it photography, video, painting – our mirrored reflection is not a thing created – not at least in the common sense of creativity that we associate with form-making. A self-portrait, to give one obvious example, will take time, effort and skill. Our mirror image usually involves nothing of that. There is no complex intentionality or elaborate act of creation; there is only light and a humble piece of glass. The mirror images that occur on the mirror's surface are not made and do not change. Unlike other images they cannot be classified according to period, convention, technique or style. Mirror images do not have a history and cannot be subject of iconographic analysis or critique. They cannot be destroyed or become the object of iconoclastic polemics. Mirror images have form but no prescribed aesthetic; they have visual content but no meaning. Lacking a tangible, physical presence also means that the mirror image cannot be dated, exhibited, shared. Viewing our idol in the mirror is a transient and lonely experience. What's more, the mirroring cannot migrate to another medium; it will not be printed or broadcasted.

The mirror image provides an unmediated visual copy of what it represents. It signifies a natural occurrence. Specifically, the mirror offers a meeting place where two occurrences, that of our living body (the image referent) and that of our mirrored body (the mirror image), momentarily intertwine. One peculiar characteristic of this meeting between the mirror image and its referent is that unlike other signifying relations it is based on synchronicity and co-presence. The referent (our body) must be present for the mirror image to occur. Indeed, one of 'the most striking things about a mirror is the perfect temporal contingency between the viewing individual's movements and those of the reflection.'[4] Unlike conventional signs and images there cannot be mirror image in the absence of its causative referent. Our body reflected in the mirror is the product of theft or abduction. We may construct the mirror, and we may cause our mirroring by situating our body in front of the mirror and by turning our gaze to it, but the mirroring itself is not affected by human intention. Rather, it is the other way around. We are caught by the mirror, drawn into it. Umberto Eco also refers to the mirror as 'theft' of the image. He writes:

> The fact that the mirror image is a most peculiar case of double and has the traits of a unique case explains why mirrors inspired so much literature; this virtual duplication of stimuli (which sometimes works as if there were a duplication of both my body as an object and my body as a subject, splitting and facing itself), this theft of an image, this unceasing temptation to believe I am someone else, makes man's experience with mirrors an absolutely unique one, on the threshold between perception and signification.[5]

The self-contradictory character of the mirror image has always been something of a paradox. The ambivalent ontology of the mirror image, being and at the same time not-being, has been the main source of its enchantment as a mode of representation. It is also why most people tacitly assume that mirroring is the kind of imagery best described by optics rather than by aesthetics or semiotics. From one particular point of view, the mirror image offers a paradigm case of mimicry: trivial as it may be the image that we generate intentionally (standing in front of our mirror) or unintentionally (passing by a shop's window) is accurate and alive as an image can be. From another point of view, the mirror image appears the most elusive image of all: a phantom, leaving behind no memory or any other material trace.

It appears then that our engagement with the mirror, and the product of this engagement, eludes our familiar taxonomies and categories. Apparently, the mirroring lacks the usual traits we associate with other images and types of imagery. Indeed, if images, as William Mitchell notes, are 'enigmas … prison houses which lock the understanding away from the world,'[6] then the mirroring is even more so. How are we to get a better sense of the mirroring in the face of its distinctive qualities? It seems it's not enough to ask just what is it. Best if we ask also: what does it 'do'? How does it 'behave'? It is on the social and psychological levels that mirrors reveal their true power. The moment we turn our gaze at their surface mirrors become instruments of an existential sort. Allowing us to gaze at the reflected image of ourselves, mirrors are turned into what the philosopher Michel Foucault describes as technologies of the self.[7] We propose there are at least three distinctive ways by which the mirror-gazing experience achieves its impact: by lying to us, by mimicking our actions and by clinging on stubbornly to a sort of pre-modern enchantment.

Liar, trickster, mime

Let's start with the first of those mannerisms, the *lying to us*. Here lies a paradox. We trust the mirror. Once we come to know how it works as a reflective surface we formulate a belief that the mirror image cannot lie: what we see inside the mirror replicates what exists on the outside world. As human beings equipped with the power of imagination we are able to think the impossible, to think of what cannot exist and cannot be real. But nothing 'unreal' or 'non-existent' can have a mirror image. Borrowing again the words of Umberto Eco: 'A mirror does not "translate"; it records what struck it just as it is struck. It tells the truth to an inhuman extent, as it is well known by those who – facing a mirror – cannot any longer deceive themselves about their freshness. Our brain interprets retinal data; a mirror does not interpret an object.'[8] Still, contrary to what we believe the mirror greets us with a distortion of reality. Do you remember Gombrich's experiment from the Introduction? If you do, then you may recall that the virtual face we look at in our mirror is half the size of our real head. The reason for the misconception is simple: the mirror is always placed half way between us and our reflection. Notwithstanding our common misconception about the size of our looking-glass face, we are also harbouring wrong beliefs on how the size of a mirroring is affected by our position in relation to the mirror. As studies in optics have repeatedly demonstrated, we have indeed a very poor understanding of images on mirror[9] and the way we predict or perceive them. Indeed, most of us are unaware of how or when the mirror makes something visible.

This misapprehension is not entirely our fault. Mirrors are 'uncanny at a basic physical and experiential level'.[10] In the simplest of words mirrors are tricksters: illusionist devices. The illusion of transparency that they give is the exact opposite of what they really are. Made by various materials (polished metal surfaces or silver glass), the mirror's main characteristic is an almost total non-absorption of light. Mirrors are actually perfectly opaque objects, usually flat and polished, which reflect light. In physical terms, mirrors are obstacles to light. Unlike the photographic camera that is made to capture light, mirrors obstruct it. Specifically, mirrors invert light's direction in space but maintain its structure so we still perceive the optic array.[11] Because of that mirrors are extremely useful epistemic objects and prosthetic means, used for many purposes – microscopes, telescopes or surgical equipment. However, in this book we are especially concerned with the role mirrors play as instruments for the acquisition of self-knowledge. In this context, mirrors are better understood as objects of visual and perceptual trickery, sympathy and affect. Mirrors have been lying to us so loudly and for so long that the lie has become invisible. Even as we know that mirrors are perfectly opaque when they appear transparent or that our mirroring is half the size of our real body, we still refuse to see it. We are, it seems, unable to become aware of the mirror's illusion. What's more, we do not care. We find little interest in the fact that the mirror reflects what we are not: flat images on glass.

Phantomachia

As we said, one distinctive feature of the mirror image is that it appears as 'alive' as an image can be. But whatever is that we see in the mirror will certainly perish as soon as our physical self walks away. Contrary to other forms and media of representation our self-image will never find a permanent 'rescue' in the looking-glass; it cannot be viewed again in the future, like a portrait or a photograph. The mirroring is a mortal image. To paraphrase Jacques Derrida, the mirror does not allow our ghosts to re-emerge. The phantom in the mirror has nothing to do with the future; we cannot call it back. What does this mean?

In the 1983 film *Ghost Dance* (directed by Ken McMullen), we watch Derrida declaring himself to be a ghost. Ghosts speak through him, he says, and play his role. 'The cinema is the art of ghosts, a battle of phantoms'.[12] There is a paradox: cinematography enhances the influence of ghosts, while it should have diminished it, like modern technologies usually do. Indeed, contrary to a mirror, a film gives images the ability to endlessly reappear. The cinematic image becomes thus the living image and participates in a 'phantomachia': a battle of images. Cinema is 'the art of allowing ghosts to come back'.[13] To be in a film, for Derrida, is to become a ghost: an image and a voice that will haunt us in the future.

The mirror, however, does not have the power to bring back the dead; it does not present us with an opportunity of a technical 'afterlife'. The mirror image will not come back to haunt us or extend into the future. It will die immediately and without a trace the moment we will walk away from the mirror. The mirror has no language. Neither sounds nor images of the past are transmitted through the mirror to distant places and distant people – like a mime the mirroring is a silent, rooted presence. But there is still a battle involved: that of the real body and the body in the mirror. The body in the mirror appears living. It becomes a living phantom. Mimicry is a compelling characteristic of the mirror image. It gives to it the illusion of life. It is also an illusion we can maintain for as long as we want. The experience of mirror gazing does not end abruptly by pressing the stop button on our video recorder or with the photographic camera's clicking sound. Time is not arrested in front of a mirror. It is lived through. The mirror double not only changes posture and moves (like images in film) but it does so in front of us, mimicking, unfailingly, the present tense of our physical self. The 're-presentational mobility'[14] of the mirroring is of a distinctive kind. Mimicry invests the mirror image with verisimilitude; it renders it more 'alive' than any other image, enabling it, thus, to compete with life in the present tense.

The mirror presents us with a perfect illusion of bilocation,[15] that is, the feeling of being present in more than one place at a time. It challenges life as it happens. The 'phantomachia' is of a different kind: the mirror does not allow the past image to invade the present. The 'threat', the antagonism of the mirror phantom is directly upon our living body and upon the breathing moment. Similarly, the journey the mirror affords us is not from past to present, or present to future like in film, but one of bilocation, of seeing an image of us outside of our bodies. Looking in the mirror, therefore, is a travel from 'here' (in front of the mirror) to 'there' (on the glass) which does not translate into reality. Yet, as our mirrored self shifts or smiles back to us, our genuine, perceptual intuition concerning what we are seeing is clouded. Contrary to a self-portrait or photograph, the apparent synchronicity of the reproduction of the mirror image with our attempt (we see our mirror self 'acting' with us) enhances the mirror's 're-presentational illusion',[16] suspending our usual perceptual routines of making sense of the world. The mirroring does not await us inside a family photo album, framed on the wall, or 'saved' in the digital memory of our computer. The life of the mirror image depends on us. It is there to meet us whenever we look in the mirror; we leave and it vanishes.

The terror of bilocation

The ability to gaze into our own eyes is, of course, a prosthetic ability rather than a feature of human naked biological endowment. Our shadow-self in the mirror might make us feel ill at ease: the mirror reflects unfailingly what our bodies were not made to see – not in a blurry, lake-like manner, but in a crystal-clear visible illusion. We are, of course, perfectly familiar with looking at our reflection, with seeing virtual, mirrored selves. Still, there remains an oddity: a split between 'I' and 'me',[17] between our physical self and our self-image. According to Ronald Barthes, before the invention of photography,[18] the vision of our photographic double had been a major source of enchantment often related to hallucinosis. 'But today', he argues, 'it is as if we repressed the profound madness of Photography: it reminds us of its mythic heritage only by that faint uneasiness which seizes me when I look at "myself" on a piece of paper.'[19]

The mirror image can also be profoundly unsettling, perhaps even more than photography, as we will have the chance to illustrate in a variety of cases. Of course, most people are perfectly accustomed with the mirror. We have learned to forget and repress the profound madness of the mirror as well. Still, even more than the photographic image, the mirroring, with its aptitude for live mimicry, often reminds us something of the original unease and fear that the experience of seeing our double outside of our bodies always embodies. The presence of the mirror, our knowledge of this artefact, matches the vision with reasonable explanation. Nevertheless, staring at our staring face may become, after a while, uncomfortable.

To understand better the affective power of the mirror image and the disquiet associated with it, we will, for a while, take the mirror away: it is going to be us and our mirror double without the reassuring presence of the looking-glass. How would such an experience be described? In psychiatric terms, the encounter with one's double correlates with the well-known disorder of autoscopy – a term coined by the Greek words 'autos' (self) and 'skopeo' (looking at). Autoscopic phenomena are illusory visual experiences defined by the perception of the images of one's own body or one's face within space, either from an internal point of view, as in a mirror, or from an external point of view.[20] The perception of one's exact double is often referred to as the mirror hallucination. Also interesting is negative heautoscopy that describes the inability to find one's reflection in the mirror, and heautoscopic echropraxia that refers to the perception of our double imitating our movements. Autoscopic experiences feel real entailing, often, a sense of strangeness towards one's body. There is no clear indication of the duration of the phenomena; it might take minutes, hours, or sometimes an illusionary double might be the steady companion of a patient. Importantly, the experience of autoscopy is mostly associated with feelings of absolute terror and shock that sometimes lead to repeated suicide attempts. Franscesca Anzellotti and her colleagues discuss the experience of a forty-year-old epileptic woman suffering from depression and heautoscopic seizures. At times, during the heautoscopic episodes she describes seeing an image of her body in normal size in front of her as if looking in a mirror. The disturbing vision would be mimicking her actions or be holding the same objects she was holding. The patient's double would appear at random, whether she was at home or outside working, provoking a feeling of dissociation between her body and mind. The patient described the chronic demoralizing effect of the experience and attributed to it two attempted suicides. She claimed to be aware of her autoscopic body's words and thoughts and that the 'experience of bilocation was petrifying and shocking'.[21] But no matter the degree of fear and uneasiness, the encounter with one's double, with a 'doppelganger',[22] is always confusing. Patients often report to locate themselves in the position of their illusionary mirroring, while a sensation of detachment of one's body and vertigo may also be involved.

It is no wonder that the vision of our double can be absolutely terrifying. The relevant phenomena from psychopathology help to illustrate the profound alterity that the experience of our mirror image as a form of bilocation often entails. To various degrees, this profound alterity is something we all have briefly experienced, when as small children we went through our own personal initiation rites of mirror self-recognition. It is, however, in those rare anthropological occasions that we are offered the opportunity to capture similar existential transitions in small, and still unhabituated, communities (unaccustomed to mirrors and self-images) that the fear of self-bilocation can be observed in its natural context.

We can witness one of those rare ethnographic instances following the anthropologist Edmund Carpenter to the territory of Papua New Guinea in the South West Pacific. Carpenter, a forerunner in visual anthropology and a close collaborator of media theorist Marshall McLuhan,[23] found himself in an extraordinary place. During the period of his study (1969–1970), Papua New Guinea was still one of those unique territories where for many people 'the steel axe, transistor radio, and camera arrived together'.[24] As Carpenter characteristically observes: 'Port Moresby, the capital of the eastern section, resembles a southern Californian town with air-conditioned buildings, supermarkets, and a drive-in theatre. Four hundred miles to the west, tiny isolated bands practice cannibalism. The bulk of the population lies between these extremes, living in thousands of tiny villages and speaking over 700 different languages.'[25] Back then, the territory of Papua New Guinea was also in the process of becoming independent as a sovereign country. Modern media like radio and film was about to reach, for the first time, this amazing mixture of local communities and cultures. Carpenter was hired as a communication consultant to help understand better the usage and the actual impact that the introduction and spread of new media would have had on the isolated tribes living in small bands on mountains, swamps and islands. He relished on the opportunity to study the reaction of people who had never seen a whole reflection of themselves in a mirror or camera – hardly a visual anthropologist could have hoped for more interesting fieldwork.

What happens, Carpenter wondered, 'when a person – for the first time – sees himself in a mirror, in a photograph, on a screen'?[26] One of the isolated tribes that Carpenter had the opportunity to study was the Biami of the Papuan

Plateau. The Biami tribe lived in a place of murky rivers and were otherwise unfamiliar with any metallic or slate-reflecting surfaces. Carpenter reports the existence of coin-sized scraps of mirrors, too small to give self-reflections and valued only as light reflectors.[27] As one may have expected, eyes innocent to the specular image would experience dissonance and confusion. But in this instance what Carpenter observed seems more radical. Carpenter describes the reaction of the people of the Biami tribe to the mirror as one of acute anxiety, confusion and terror; emotions very similar to those experienced by patients suffering episodes of autoscopic hallucination. In Carpenter's words: 'They were paralysed: after the first startled response – covering their mouth and ducking their heads – they stood transfixed, staring at their images, only their stomach muscles betraying their tension.'[28] Unable to move, the anxiety of Carpenter's subjects became evident only by their trembling bodies. 'It's as if they had vomited up an organ: they cover their mouth and duck their heads, almost as a delayed reflex, trying to prevent this.'[29]

What was the cause of this 'not ordinary fear?'[30] According to Cameron's interpretation, the mirror image exposed a second 'symbolic' self to the subjects, one that being outside of their bodies and the protected space of the physical self, was made public and vulnerable. Of course, this challenge to self-localization was only temporary. Habit, it seems, alleviates the terror of bilocation – or masks it into a faint uneasiness. The members of the Biami tribe, after a few days of contact with the mirror, were seen grooming themselves casually in front of it. 'When mirrors become a part of daily life, it's easy to forget how frightening self-discovery, self-awareness can be.'[31] Habit eliminates the frightening and mesmerizing qualities of mirroring. Unfortunately, it also dampens our curiosity and the wonder of self-discovery.

This brings us to another important point in our discussion. Some forms of everyday technology retain the power to enchant us into seeing the world in a more magical form. The anthropologist Alfred Gell writes that the 'enchantment of technology' which is inherent in all kinds of technical processes[32] is a force that influences our emotions and behaviour – mainly by making us act in a manner incomprehensible. Of course, given the right context, technology can also have the opposite effect, disenchanting our ways of seeing and making sense of the world. The mirror is one of those boundary objects of everyday magic and science that carries the promise of uniting reality and imagination.

It delivers on that promise in a direct and powerful way as it presents us with a universe where looking at our double is possible, scientifically explainable, and therefore, safe. But even though habit takes away the terror of bilocation, it does not take away the allure; the uneasiness that lurks beneath our encounter with our double or the mesmerizing effect that goes with it. Mirror's enchantment primarily emanates from its distinctive ability to integrate within the same temporal framework a series of causal transactions that encompass aesthetical and magical elements. Unlike other images and representational media the captivating power of the mirror, as a technology of enchantment, does not stem from its ability to serve as an index of technical efficacy; rather, it primarily emanates from the suggested intertwining of the lived phenomenal body and its visible synchronous representation on the mirror's surface. With mirroring the image or our self is both presented and re-presented.

Vanishing act

The double in the mirror is a great illusionist. Our mirrored self ensnares us in the way that a hunter disguises his or herself to mimic the appearance of the prey animal (we discuss this extensively in Chapter 7). The mirror double doesn't just lure us with mimicry; it also eliminates its own medium: the mirror. It is always the mirror image that we focus on. The mirror itself becomes invisible; no one is looking at it. The medium does fall victim to its product. This is because, unlike other images, the mirror image 'borrows' something of our life energy. So, when we talk about our relationship with the mirror we mostly mean our relationship with our reflection. We describe our perception, behaviour and emotion towards it. The moment in which our body becomes visible in the glass is the moment where the mirror 'vanishes'.

Mirrors change the way we see. They dictate what secret parts of us are visible. The double that appears in it is an actor that always plays 'us'. It mimics our every move. It is made in our image. But it has no history, it carries no memory and it has no life of its own. The mirror image has a place among the family of images that is uncertain and always under dispute. It lacks material traces – thus it is elusive and fleeting. It is accessible to everyone – thus it is cheap and readily available. It makes our bodies visible – thus it is important and unique. In the end, the mirroring is both precious and trivial. We cannot clearly classify or easily describe it, but there is – and we have all felt it – a kind of pressing demand on it, because of it we ask the most private question: we ask of it to tell us who we are.

Remember that the paradox of mirroring is that, in one important sense, the mirror image always tells the truth. As Eco remarks, one 'cannot lie with and through a mirror image'.[33] Instinctively, and rather naively, we perceive our mirroring as a sort of 'us': we are what we see in the mirror. And yet, to put our mirrored self back where it belongs – in the inanimate sphere of optic images – it only takes a gesture. All we have to do is raise our hand and try to touch our mirror face. Naturally, the spell is broken. The sense of the cold glass on our fingers provides us with the absolute limit of our habitual, warm body. Our eyes, somehow, now stare at our hand: we are not what we look like. Doing this exercise might at first seem strange: what can be said about our mirrored bodies if we are not allowed to talk about visual appearances, forms and representations? In that case, the resulting story would be of a mirror gaze capable of bypassing appearances. A gaze that will probably lead each one of us to different paths – all of them useful and worth exploring. In the following chapters we explore some possible ways (out of many) to think about the life of the mirror image. It is for each reader to decide where exactly this might lead.

Beautiful scars

'Give me the glass, and therein will I read.'

William Shakespeare, *Richard II*

The gaze of the holy inquisition

Not a long time ago a friend shared with us a curious experience. Her story opens like a farce: a lady walks into the beauty department of a popular high-street shop. She looks around at products but without a clear intention to buy. A young shopping assistant approaches and politely recommends a very effective (and considerably expensive) cosmetic product: one with 'real powers to battle ageing and help, particularly, with those deep wrinkles on the forehead'. This is uncomfortable news to the lady in the shop. Dismissively, and rather naively, she suggests that she doesn't need that product simply because she does not have deep wrinkles on her forehead.

What does the vendor do?

She smiles knowingly and disappears under the counter for a short second only to re-emerge, armed this time, with a huge ×10 magnifying mirror mounted in a round frame, and fully equipped with a polished red handle. To understand what is to follow, we first take a moment to appreciate the thing called the magnifying mirror. As the name suggests, it is a lens used to present an enlarged reflection of an object. It has a curved reflecting surface and many different applications – most of them very useful to humankind. Like any other mirror, its main job is to reflect light. A magnifying mirror, or a concave spherical mirror, however, concentrates the light it reflects, directing all rays into a central focus point. As a human face gets within the focal length of the mirror, the reflecting light diverges, producing a magnified image. The aim of the magnifying mirror is usually to allow one to inspect parts of one's face – not to offer a realistic and complete face reflection. To achieve that aim, one must preferably face the mirror head on and not at an angle. Thus, the magnifying mirror of our story was placed directly in front of our friend's face, and at a very close distance, like an inescapable object of destiny. Then, our friend was kindly invited to take a good look specifically at her forehead and reconsider her situation.

She did.

And she reconsidered.

Describing her forehead to us afterwards, she announced that it resembles verses of T. S. Eliot's *The Wasteland*. She said that, in that mirror, her skin was full of cracks and craters, veins pink and blue, deep wrinkles and deeper ones. To summarize, our friend bought the expensive beauty product suggested to her by the mirror-yielding vendor. The product failed on its promise. But why did the enhanced visibility of lines and wriggles produce such a dramatic effect? Laura Clarke and Meridith Griffin speak of an irony very much to the point: 'the irony of the women's perceptions of being invisible as a result of their visibly aged appearances'.[1] That is, as signs of ageing become visible on their skins, women, as well as men, might start to fear they will become socially invisible. Understandably, having a mirror which will allow you to gaze on facial blemishes next to anti-ageing products enables beauty industry to immediately capitalize on that fear. Now, a magnifying mirror that would enlarge ten times the visibility of the signs of ageing would boost the concern of looking older accordingly. Not a bad idea for making profit. Still, there is a paradox: according to Clarke and Griffin, available beauty work instead of enhancing women's appearance and social value end up highlighting ageist conceptions. Women, even though aware of the discrimination and ageism, have no other option but to submit to the prevailing ideology and try to mask their age by the use of beauty products and cosmetic procedures: 'That women engage in beauty work suggests that regardless of their awareness or their agency, their choices are ultimately determined in a world where to challenge ageist stereotypes is to run the risk of further stigmatisation and permanent invisibility.'[2]

The mirror inspection was a test. Our friend in the beauty shop was forced to evaluate herself against an enlarged mirror image of her face: a larger-than-life reflection that not only did not resemble her but could hardly qualify as human.

The very attempt, of course, was absurd: our friend's forehead stood no chance. And yet, in that 'mirror trial' the magnifying mirror had taken the role of both prosecutor and judge in a peculiar holy inquisition against the heresy of ageing skin. The mirror's relationship to the person gazing in it was one of power, grounded in the way society or institutions practice control through steered judgements, regulating, for that purpose, human thoughts, senses and action. In our case, the sense manipulated was sight: the way one gazes and perceives one's face in the mirror. The gaze was directed in a dexterous manner towards the centre of a magnifying glass to meet not a habitual self-image but a face fragmented into exaggerated parts. Consequently, the face was constructed by the person holding the mirror – it was a face invented. It was also a face exhibited.

In front of the indisputable evidence of the magnifying mirror the lady of our story turned into the most fervent judge of herself. Yet, it was not just the magnifying mirror. It was the gaze she cast in it: a tyrannical and incriminating gaze we call, with some liberty, the gaze of the holy inquisition, because one can only be found guilty by it. Either we look in a magnifying mirror, a regular one, or even at each other, the gaze reduces the body in its parts – forehead, eyes, nose, lips, cheeks, chin, ears, neck, hands, etc. Then, it puts blame on them. The gaze has even invented phrases to name and shame: 'crows-feet' for the skin around the eyes, 'eleven lines' for the bit between the eyebrows, 'marionette lines' for the lines next to our lips, 'turtle neck', 'bingo-wings' for our arms, 'muffin-top' for our waists, 'cottage-cheese legs', 'snake-nest' for the veins on hands and feet and many more. The aim is to demean, hurt and objectify people of a certain age or weight into submission. Young and beautiful bodies, on the other hand, are 'voraciously publicized and consumed by popular culture'.[3] The gaze of the holy inquisition produces a mirror reflection which is virtually unwatchable for the great majority of people, while obsessively stalking its young and attractive victims. 'Institutionalized gazing at youth, for example in mass media, is underpinned by the cultural assumption that physical beauty itself is premised on youthfulness and denied to older people.'[4] Being convinced that to feel happy and lovable you must look young and sexually attractive produces a serious conflict between person and mirror and undermines self-identity: not looking young becomes not looking like your 'true self' which is hidden somewhere within old skin and is realized as 'a state in which the body is in opposition to the self'.[5] Under these terms, one could end up feeling alienated from one's mirrored body. Gaining knowledge and self-awareness from mirror gazing becomes unlikely, while looking in the mirror alone might turn into a painful experience.[6]

To look in the mirror is to ask for a story. There are many things we could ask for the mirror to tell us. Mirror gazing solely for the purpose of evaluating one's beauty and youthfulness, however, limits the collaborating narrative between mirror and mirror observer. In other words, beauty affords only one question, while the mirror is capable of answering plenty. The mirror, in fact, is a great storyteller. Although it does not speak, it draws stories out of our minds. It makes a storyteller out of us all. The stories relate to how we interpret our mirror image; how we treat it and put it into words. Indeed, we can 'read' the mirror in many different ways, none of which representing an absolute and only truth. It all depends on the way we look in it. As with any other aspect of visual experience, what we see in the mirror is always mediated: 'The way we see things is affected by what we know or what we believe.'[7] The lady we described staring into a magnifying glass in the beginning of our chapter, for instance, inspected her mirror image from a specific point of view, afforded by the beauty industry. Her gaze has been directed and exploited for profit. Consequently, the story she made about herself had to do with the lack of an idealized, smooth and unwrinkled mirrored face.

In the absence of an alternative way of looking in the mirror, the lady in the beauty shop was left desperate about her appearance and, in a way, disappointed of herself. 'Personal narrative emerges out of experience while giving shape to it.'[8] In the case of mirror gazing, the mirrored self becomes the centre around which our narrative develops. Inevitably, what we 'shape' with our narrative is our self. As consumer society censors and gives negative meanings to ageing skin, our ageing skin in the mirror is perceived 'as the source of those meanings.'[9] The body in the mirror, in other words, cannot be separated from the propaganda built around it and is looked at as the original source of the observer's frustration. The mirror, thus, turns into a distorting lens, an oppressive device for mistreating the self. Our friend describing her skin as a *Wasteland* is a good indication for Kathleen Woodward's 'horror of the mirror image',[10] the experience of abhorring our mirrored self.

It is often the case that, in order to feel the need to buy things, the stories we tell ourselves while we gaze in the mirror would better be sad. Clearly, no person content in their image would go out searching for expensive skin treatments. Beauty industry is colossal and to remain profitable customers should continue to associate lines and blemishes on their skin with feelings of misery and failure. This attitude is maintained and reinforced by an incessant stream of advertising which relates unrealistic, retouched images of perfect skin to a narrative of being happy, accepted and desired. It is a narrative of need which makes us think that something is missing.[11] It is also a fake narrative against which we are invited to evaluate our mirroring. In reality, of course, we are not invited to truly investigate our appearance in the mirror. We are simply tricked into verifying the natural fact of growing older that equals our inadequacy: our sharp contrast to the prevailing myth of eternal youth. Thus, in the hands of the beauty and fashion industry, the mirror, through no fault of its own, is transformed from an instrument of self-awareness into a tool of oppression. But what exactly is it asked of the mirror viewer to achieve in order to be happy?

A desire that can only look at itself

Advertising campaigns, apart from determining how we should look like, are taking the extra step of putting their words into our minds.[12] To do so they come up with slogans, some of which become famous and stay in our heads like forced incantations promoting a certain way of thinking, and therefore, a way of seeing. L'Oréal's successful slogan 'because I'm worth it' is a good case in point. According to philosopher Simon Blackburn, one can hardly find a better example to illustrate the mindset of a person self-absorbed, vain and arrogant – a person on an imaginary pedestal uncaring for the rest of the world.[13] The promise communicated to the viewer is that they too can live on a pedestal, forever enjoying the admiration and worship of the rest of humanity if only they use L'Oréal products. So the 'you're worth it', motto, simple and seemingly harmless turns, in their minds, into 'you aren't worth it', not yet. "'I myself am but a poor worm," thinks the victim, "with warts and fat and farts and fears. But L'Oréal will waft me away, take me up to the empyrean, the other world where the royalty – no, the gods – live free from mortal woes and flaws and worries …'"[14]

Now, let's wake up.

In the real world, L'Oréal's (or any other company's) cosmetic products could never deliver on their promise for perfect skin. On the contrary, the constant self-examining gaze promoted by advertising campaigns would make the potential customer feel less beautiful and loved than they really are. Not only are people's expectations manipulated by advertising but their imagination as well: readymade images of what is beautiful dominate and obscure our own aesthetic practices and choices. Advertising slogans like the 'because I am worth it' motto creep into our minds and then springs up in our everyday lives as something acceptable and satisfying. It even becomes our voice: a legitimate phrase we might repeat to others or, more importantly, to ourselves. And when we gaze at our mirrored reflection the story we make about our appearance, attractiveness and self-worth is not our own but intrusive echoes of the mainstream propaganda. Like in a state of hypnosis, to use the words of Marshall McLuhan, '[w]e have become so groggy, so passive, so helpless, amidst the endless barrage of appeals that "we go about our business," as we say. But the business of the advertiser is to see that we go about our business with some magic spell or tune or slogan throbbing quietly in the background of our mind ...'[15]

Our mirror gaze, in the end, is colonized. Our memory resembles a piece of paper so overwritten with slogans that no words of our own can ever find space: our ability to 'author' ourselves in front of the mirror is compromised. Of course, we are all more or less aware of the false promises of advertising. The digital tricks responsible for the images we see on visual media are not much of a secret, and, to be fair, more often than not the context of advertisements is so profoundly exaggerated one might wonder how we actually fall for it.

Still, we all fall for it, to some degree. And like it is the case with Gombrich's experiment we mentioned in the introduction – where circling the outline of our mirrored reflection we find it to be much smaller than our true body – we do not bother ourselves with it. It seems we are harbouring under the illusion that, being aware of its tricks, our minds are protected, impervious to the propaganda of consumer culture. Yet, a prerequisite of finding our way through the hypnotic forest of advertising slogans (along with their accompanying melodies and jingles) to a silent place where we can create our own stories, is to accept the fact that we are not immune to the toxic and self-altering environment of advertising. This denial, '[t]he myth of immunity from persuasion may do more to protect self-respect than accurately comprehend the subtleties and implications of influence'.[16]

Clearly, not many of us would ever admit in believing the context of advertising and even fewer would fail to acknowledge the irrational and blown-up statements made by advertisers. Even 'the creators of advertising can claim that no one takes it all very seriously; it is more or less in fun. The viewer can adopt a similar attitude. The viewer's self-respect requires a rejection on the conscious level along with some ridicule. Beneath the ridicule the commercial does its work'.[17] A self-assuring attitude alone cannot block the influence of advertiser's narratives. On the contrary, it has granted the advertisers more space. All the ads around us – on the internet and social media, on TV, on buses, on buildings, on bus stops, in magazines, in shopping malls, in subway stations – are now so omnipresent and inescapable they have become our environment. In that environment our desire is directed and manipulated. It is polluted by slogans. It is reduced to praise-seeking. It becomes self-absorbed. A desire that can only look at itself. In the end it becomes a mere feeling of need.

The mirroring of disgust

If we fail to create a personal narrative in front of the mirror, we will be left with the ones dictated to us. We might also begin to mimic the images we receive through advertising, just like our mirror reflection unfailingly mimics us. As Bernard Stiegler writes, ' a huge proportion of the population is totally subjected to the aesthetic *conditioning* of marketing, now hegemonic for a vast majority of the world, and is, therefore estranged from any *experience* of aesthetic investigation'.[18]

So, the question is: do we really explore our options on how to appear in the mirror or do we, somehow, take it on faith? Is mirror gazing for us an experience of 'aesthetic investigation'? We have said many times that advertisers are trying to control our emotions and manipulate our desire. Here it is in the very words of an American advertising agency: 'what makes this country (North America) great is the creation of needs and desires, the creation of disgust for everything that is old and unfashionable.'[19] Top marks then to the advertisers for the 'great countries' and the disgust that they create. But, when it comes to mirror gazing, the 'old and unfashionable' that we are schooled to be disgusted by might include our bodies. So, what are we to do to escape the feelings of lack and disgust the advertising industry is so proud of generating? How can we ignore the idiotic and potentially painful propaganda?

Sadly, we cannot. At least, not the great majority of us without the iron will of an ascetic. For the rest of us it will take some serious effort. It will not happen spontaneously. As Erica Reischer and Kathryn Koo point out:

> Despite our ability to theorize, analyze, and contextualize the underlying meaning of beauty in contemporary culture, we are no less enthralled by its display … As much as we find solace in well-worn adages that 'beauty is only skin deep' and 'beauty is in the eye of the beholder', our daily experience in the social world, and even our own responses to the body beautiful, tell us otherwise.[20]

Yes, beauty is usually culturally constructed. It changes from place to place and through time, but beauty is important.

> We are a self-conscious species. We struggle for social acceptance and inclusion by endless attempts at influencing what others see in us, think of us, represent of us. It is an all-too-human propensity that cuts across people and cultures. We are obsessed with the idea of what is public about us, obsessed with the representation other people might have of us …'[21]

The need to be accepted and loved by others is a perfectly human characteristic. According to Philippe Rochat, without others 'we would not be. As infants we would not have survived. As adults, we would not have any explicit sense of who we are; we would have no ability, nor any inclination to be self-conscious.'[22]

The mirror is a constant reminder of the eye of the other. As such, it is constantly recruited in advertising. The pattern is more or less the same. At first, the mirror reflects the sad faces of people who do not like what they see in it. And then, the well-expected twist: the previously miserable faces turn into triumphant ones, after having bought and used the right product. In some ads the models are even broadcasted initially to be hiding from the mirror as if afraid of the confrontation, but after whatever is advertised has been purchased, the models appear to have suddenly become empowered, confident and ready to win the 'mirror-battle'.

The promise of victory against the mirror is, by definition, empty. Advertising is not out there to keep any promises – content and confident people would make lousy consumers. Still, longing continuously for the joyous and perfect environment of advertising we are somehow predisposed to dislike our own. In this way, it is not easy to look sympathetically in the mirror or at each other. A community of people, Stiegler notes is a community of feeling. If we are unable to love things together (landscapes, towns, objects, images, etc.), then we cannot love ourselves. 'Being together', claims the writer, 'is feeling together'.[23] If a community of people is indeed defined by a common aesthetic ground, then, perhaps our community of fake images and forced consumerism is unable to gaze itself in the mirror. Instead of loving and appreciating things together, and consequently loving ourselves, we are coached to do the opposite: we are trained to look at each other and in the mirror with disregard, creating, unfailingly, a culture of discontent.

Resistance

Should we avoid the mirror altogether? 'The fear of social rejection is the mother of all fears', Rochat wrote.[24] Would banning the mirror result in less insecurity and fear? Even though excessively looking in the mirror might not be healthy, a total ban on our self-reflection does not seem like an ideal or a practical solution either. 'Looking at ourselves in the mirror forces us to repeatedly come to terms with who we are, even though we continually change. This process of "mirroring" is in fact a central and inherent part of "being in the world," since it helps us through life to synchronize the reciprocal interaction between the outer world and ourselves'.[25] Creating a self-identity without a mirror is not easily imagined. A modern society lacking mirrors is a distant fantasy. After all, 'a significant portion of human culture is based on the reflected visibility of the personal self'.[26]

Demonizing the mirror is easy. Yet, our lack of skill in dealing with our mirroring is not the mirror's fault. Depriving ourselves from knowing our self-reflection cannot be helpful in our journey to find and care for ourselves. 'One cannot care for self without knowledge. The care for self is of course knowledge of self.'[27] Indeed, the mirror is a vital ally in finding oneself. But we do have to escape the patronizing story of how we should appear in the looking-glass. The story begins and ends with youth and beauty, at least for the vast majority of advertisers and editors of beauty and life-style magazines. If we do not possess either of the two we should be made to believe that we are irrelevant. Life and experience are, in a sense, censored. In fact, the stories advertisers and editors made are censored as well.

> Thirty-five-thousand dollars' worth of advertising was withdrawn from a British magazine the day after the editor, Carol Sarler, was quoted as saying that she found it hard to show women looking intelligent when they were plastered with makeup. A grey-haired editor for a leading women's magazine told a grey haired writer, Mary Kay Blakely, that an article about the glories of grey hair cost her magazine the Clairol account for six months.[28]

The censorship extends to the images of older women. Naomi Wolf quotes a director of *Life Magazine*, Bob Ciano, admitting that all female images are retouched. That goes also for 'well-known [older] women who doesn't want to be retouched'.[29] There is not even a choice for women to show their true image to the public. This, of course, results in ignorant and manipulated readers that as Dalma Heyn, editor of two women's magazines, mentions in Wolf's book have no idea what a real woman's face looks like.[30] Our relationship with the mirror is deeply affected: '60-year-old readers look in the mirror and think they look too old, because they are comparing themselves to some retouched face smiling back at them from a magazine'.[31] The issue is more serious than it may at first appear. 'It's about the freedom to imagine one's own future, to be proud of one's life. Airbrushing women's face has the same political echo that would resound if all positive images of blacks were routinely lightened.'[32]

Advice that women read in women's magazines concerning cosmetic products are totally untrustworthy. 'Women's magazines transmit "information" about beauty products in a heavily self-censored medium. When you read about skin creams and holy oils, you are not reading free speech. Beauty editors are unable to tell the truth about their advertiser's products. In Harper's Bazar article "Younger every Day", opinions on various anti-aging creams were solicited only and entirely from the presidents of ten cosmetic companies.'[33]

Unfortunately, as Naomi Wolf correctly points out: 'The healthier the industry, the sicker are women's consumer and civil rights…. The woman who buys a product on the recommendation of beauty copy is paying for the privilege of being lied to by two sources.'[34]

Somehow, we are supposed to accept the situation and not make a fuss about being lied to. But since docilely accepting deceit does not sound like a brilliant idea, how should we respond? This is not an easy challenge. You see, a story will always 'appear' in the looking-glass, along with our reflection. A story that explains us and puts our bodies into words. We share our life stories with the mirror, like we share body memory with our bicycle.[35] And we all act into the world with our bodies. To paraphrase Merleau-Ponty, we are conscious of our bodies through the world and of the world through our bodies.[36] 'The body', Merleau-Ponty wrote is, 'our general medium for having a world'.[37] We will always need a narrative to help us make sense of our changing bodies in any given time, and we should be making our own instead of rehearsing, like a good student, the false consciousness of the oppressed.[38] Every story that will come out of this act is a story of resistance: an antidote, in other words, to the deafening transmission of the 'ageless regime' and its manipulative fiction.

A narrative that will initiate a process of freedom.

The mirror could be put to use as a tool of resistance against the advertising 'tutorials' we endure every day, instead of being the advertiser's weapon. Mirror gazing can even amount to an act of civil disobedience (if you look in the mirror in order to prepare a face that defies the social norm). Yet, one cannot resist anything by asking the mirror if he or she is beautiful. Addressing the mirror solely with question of beauty, youth and desirability cannot produce the gaze of resistance we are after. On the contrary, it is the gaze that exists in the tale of *Snow White*, where the evil queen desperately seeks reassurance by asking her magic mirror, every day, if she is still 'the fairest of them all'. Likewise, in our image-obsessed culture we are herded to gaze in the mirror in the same way. But the beauty question is only one of the many questions we could ask the looking-glass, and it is a poor one, after all. A question doomed to eventually create a negative narrative of the self: nobody remains young and beautiful forever. To be honest, we seriously suspect that the mirror of the evil queen in the story of *Snow White* was innocent – never diminished or uttered a word back to her. The mirror is but a silent mime. What the queen was clearly hearing each day in front of the looking-glass was nothing but her own verdict. It was all in her head.

What we say to ourselves in front of the mirror is a choice. The crucial task, therefore, is not to wonder if we appear beautiful in it. 'How does a body figure on its surface the very invisibility of its hidden depth?'[39] asked Judith Butler. We ask: how do we find that hidden and invisible depth in the mirror?

In search of beauty/in defence of a scar

In certain ways, a fairy tale and the world of perfect images produced in advertising is equally imagined. According to this non-existent and yet very visible world the body should appear young looking and of an almost punishable weight.[40] The absence of lines and spots on our faces, unnatural and eventually unattainable, is the nothingness, the no-story we should all be delighted to read in our mirrors. But in the end, when it comes to narrating the self, the spotless face is an empty page. And there are more interesting stories than absence. Fascinating and imaginative narratives might spring at the interface of body and looking-glass.

What do we mean?

Let's imagine a medical setting in London. A person recovering from cosmetic surgery is presented with a mirror. The moment is thrilling. The gaze that meets the glass is one of agony – are the signs of time gone? It is really hard to tell. Certainly though, the face in the mirror seems different than before. And, with equal certainty, we can assume that for the surgery to be deemed successful the face in the mirror should appear smoother, the pain should have been minimal and evidence of the surgery (marks, scars and stitches) should be close to invisible. To smile at one's mirrored reflection there should be no obvious marks and no memory of procedure: no patient should have any recollection of how it felt like when the surgical knife cut into the skin. There is nothing for the resulting face to communicate. The face lift is to be kept a secret. Quietly, secretively, the stitched-up skin should imitate that of a younger person. The collaborative story of event, body and mirror is, therefore, one of pretence: of hide and seek.

To get to the heart of the matter we may contrast our example of cosmetic surgery with the practice of scarification. Anthropological literature abounds with a variety of techniques and narratives of this dramatic form of body modification and inscription.[41] Nuba girls of Southern Sudan, to take one example, receive their first marks on their chest, abdomen and forehead when they reach puberty. Cuts under their breasts mark the onset of menstruation. Those same cuts are later enlarged in an extensive stage of scarring which occurs after the successful weaning of the first child. Thus, the adult Nuba woman who thrived in finding a husband and in having children will have elaborate designs all over her body to show for it. Even though mainly for beauty, scars are also attained to symbolize maturity and social status and to enhance memory. In a way, they are marks that speak; marks that guide a person through their life stories and also lead and direct the behaviour of others towards that person: among the Ga'anda of Nigeria, marks on the stomach attract attention to a girl's reproductive promise. Later her forehead and forearms will receive their own scars. Waist, buttocks, base of neck, shoulder and upper arms will follow in a long process of marking life on the skin which will end with the final marking of her thighs: marks that will seal her marriage and warn other young men of her unavailability.[42] A Nuba of Southern Sudan will examine their body scars and be reminded of little triumphs: reaching adolescence, getting married, becoming warriors and hunters, birthing and breastfeeding children. Their whole life, victories and loses, pain and exultation, will be marked on their skin in elaborate designs as a map of the self. The mirror will allow them to read that map.

For another example we travel to Omdurman, a city in Sudan and Khartoum State basking under a splendid sun on the west bank of the river Nile. Anthropologist Anne Cloudsley follows the steps of a young girl who is about to have a face tattoo: the *dug al-shaloufa,* which translates as the striking of the lower lip. In a place where the custom of facial tattooing is so old that it can be seen on mummies from Merotic cemeteries that particular lip tattoo is very popular among brides-to-be.[43]

The *dug al-shaloufa* is, in our case, administered by a gypsy woman named Zaneeb. It is an arduous process. Upon arrival in Zaneeb's house, the girl lies on a mat. The tattoo artist kneels behind her trapping her face tightly between her knees: customers should not move because of the pain. Zaneeb then grabs the girl's lower lip between her fingers. She applies generously on it a mixture of powdered charcoal soaked in the gallbladder bile of a large Nile perch. She starts poking the lip with numerous needles attached together. Blood is dripping out. Zaneeb wipes it away. She puts more of her bile mixture on the girl's lips; she pokes on. The atmosphere is joyous. Friends are gathered around the girl telling jokes while holding her arms and legs firmly down so that Zaneeb would finish the job. The *dug al-shaloufa* takes approximately half an hour. The girl, like most of the customers, faints more than once. Oftentimes, future brides choose to have their upper gum tattooed as well, in which case, they are unable to eat properly for days.

According to Anne Cloudsley, only engaged women may have lip tattoo. So, with all its permanent marks and its memory of pain, the lip tattoo will forever be a visual sign of a life-changing step. Unlike what is usually promised in modern beauty clinics, the change on the woman's face, as it is the case with scarification, is intended to be boldly noticeable. Not subtle. Not painless. Not reversible. Not natural. The event we read about in Cloudsley's ethnography is collective, bloody, noisy and joyous. A loud and shared story instead of a personal, well-guarded secret.

If not deliberately muted, our bodies have a voice. Through labyrinths of marks and memory our skin puts our lives into words. From the whispers of a fine line to the screams of a scar, from the intentional tale of a tattoo to the remarkable story of birth inscribed on the body by a caesarean section, marks and wrinkles are alive, and, as one knows them intimately, constantly commutating. There are times, of course, that the marks on our bodies could speak of terrible things. But even then, the story expressed would be one of survival. Of courage and enduring life. It would be a story we've been through and should not be made to hide it. Unfortunately, in capitalist society we are constantly 'advised' to put body marks out of sight. This literally means concealing (with make-up), cutting (with surgical knives), plumping up (with fillers), paralyse (with Botox) or burning away (with lasers) the evidence of our being-in-the-world from our visible body; making, in other words, signs of our life experience – and its mirrored evidence – invisible. Here is an irony, if there ever was one: to become watchable and visible we must now erase ourselves.

Beauty industry, of course, produces an enormous amount of services and products that will not consume themselves. Constantly buying an ever-increasing array of cosmetic goods and procedures is the part we are supposed to play for the industry to be viable. Our body, however, is a magnificent storyteller and, reflected in the mirror, its stories unfold: who we are, where do we come from, how long have we been around, what have we gained and lost, what have we been up to. To erase its marks is to silence the body. There is no limit to what a body can convey through the act of gazing at it. In fact, this is what we propose to do as a mirror-gazing exercise: find a scar or a mark on our mirrored body and start a conversation with it. For instance? Well, for instance, from the sight of a scar that goes back to our childhood and was acquired falling of our bike, we can ask: what year was it? Who was our best friend then? How did we spend our days? What did we dream about? And there, in the lasting memory of a scar, we can dig out emotions and images, tears and laughter, faces, voices, sounds and smells in narrow alleys and endless summers that need that scar in order to survive.

This is how the body and the mirror create beauty. On the bare, visual realities of the mirrored skin, there is a path to the infinite riches of our lived experience that transcends the skin completely. What seems like the line of a scar transforms itself to become a line in our personal narrative and a line we can use to trace our self back to childhood: Ariadne's skein of thread.

Part Two

Re-enchantment

Looking through the looking-glass

and so, what seems to you like a
barber's basin, seems like Mambrino's helmet to me,
and it may seem like something else to another
person.

Cervantes, Don Quixote

A world that goes the wrong way

On a winter's afternoon, in one of Lewis Carroll's stories, a young girl named Alice decides to step through the drawing room's mirror and explore the world beyond it.[1] Alice has had glimpses of that world – and in particular of the 'looking-glass drawing room' as she calls the room's mirror reflection – by climbing on a chair and looking into the big mirror hung over the chimney piece. Spying like that in the mirror's depths, Alice already knows a few things about the looking-glass room. For instance, when she holds a book up to the glass the letters of the looking-glass book go the other way. Curious and excited to know more, Alice eventually climbs on the chimney piece and, as the looking-glass turns into soft silver mist, steps through it. Indeed, things on the other side of the mirror are strange: inanimate things, like chess pieces and pictures, are very much alive and instead of a bitter-cold winter's night, walking out of the looking-glass house, Alice finds herself in a spring garden.

Through the Looking-Glass and What Alice Found There, as the novel was originally published in 1871, remains to this day one of the most famous fictional endeavours to enter the mirror and glimpse at an alternate universe. So, what did Alice find there? Carroll's literary vision of the world inside the mirror is playful and outside the ordinary. It makes sense in its own unique and whimsical way. At times, that world mirrors our reality in a literary sense, as is the case with the reverse printing of the *Jabberwocky*, the looking-glass poetry book the verses of which are legible only against a mirror, or with Alice having to walk in the opposite direction of where she means to go in order to get there. But mostly, the parallels of our world and that of looking-glass are subtle and untraceable. Clearly, the looking-glass world is not just a reflection of Alice's own. This would come as a surprise to anyone expecting mirroring to be the prominent feature of a looking-glass universe. A second Alice, a double, is remarkably missing. We must now search for what is indeed there to be found.

Notably, the first thing that happens to Alice once outside the looking-glass house is to get lost. The garden's path wouldn't stay still: it twists and turns and Alice, even though trying to reach the hill, is always returning back to the house's front door. Then, Alice starts a long discussion with flowers in a flower-bed. But how does Alice mirror back to the looking-glass creatures? It is perhaps natural for Alice to suppose that she is 'normal' while the surrounding mirrored-world is extraordinary. Nevertheless, the reaction of the looking-glass creatures indicates to the contrary: the living flowers find her shape to be awkward, voices in the train suggests that Alice, having failed to provide a ticket, should be sent back as a telegram, while the red queen – a talking chess piece, to begin with – reproaches Alice for been a child without any meaning, always wrong about more or less everything and with a vicious, horrible temper. Clearly Carroll's heroine has left the world around her baffled and annoyed. If we are to accept that the way 'others *mirror* back what they see in us contributes to the self we become, subjectively and objectively',[2] then, Alice wouldn't make any sense of herself throughout her journey. Alice appears to be as alien to her new world as that world is to her. In fact, in terms of self-discovery, Alice is a hero who wonders a lot to find nothing. She enters the space of the looking-glass world with apparent ease, but cannot inhabit it – the roads seem to twist and turn on their own, most of what she says or thinks seem nonsense to other creatures. 'How I wish I was one of them!' Alice cries standing on top of a little hill, overlooking the peculiar chess-board-like country made of tiny brooks. 'I wouldn't mind being a Pawn, if only I might join – though of course I should *like* to be a Queen, best.'[3]

So Alice did not find herself. If we were to leave our analysis here, in the deep waters of self-perception, Alice's journey through the looking-glass would be an unremarkable tour in a most imaginative universe. But what if we try to see what Alice did find? That is, forget for a while the mirror's main quality of reflecting oneself and try to considerate on the possible experience of looking in the mirror not in order to see our double, but to see 'through it'. To explore the novel under this light, we will focus on the experience of being inside Carroll's world, and, purposefully, take it for granted. This approach would necessitate a restructuring of the basic question. Instead of asking what Carroll writes about Alice's journey, we ask what happens there, as if *there* really exists. In other words, we fully enter the scene and accept its terms with an intention to believe the unbelievable, willingly suspending the idea that our world (the reader's world) is real and the looking-glass world (the story's word) is fantasy – let's call this an attitude of methodological gullibility: a strategic suspension of doubt.

Crossing that line between imagination and reality, the first thing we come to realize is that certain categories – such as human and non-human, animate and inanimate – have seized to exist, or more accurately are now reconfigured. Traits and characteristics like speaking, reading, and knitting are not reserved exclusively for humans. For instance, we learn that flowers can speak very nicely. In fact, daises talk all together in shrill little voices and beetles are capable of expressing opinions. Further on in the story, the White Queen declares her unruly shawl to be out of temper and to refuse to stay where it's pinned. At the same time, humans can be seen by different species as animals, plants, or something altogether unspecified: some characters in the looking-glass world have no clue what kind of creature Alice is. A rose, nevertheless, in the garden of live flowers, seems to be quite sure that Alice is a moving flower.

Alice journeys into a world that, paradoxically, seems to have acquired a sort of a perspectival quality. We use the term 'perspectival' to describe a world 'inhabited by different sort of subjects or persons, human and non-human, which apprehend reality from distinct points of view'.[4] Brazilian anthropologist Eduardo Viveiros de Castro best expressed the notion of perspectivism in his study of the Amerindian people (see also Chapter 7). Confronted by different ideas of personhood and nonhuman agency, his ethnography portrays a world where animals or plants may be considered as persons with the ability of language and where a human or animal external form (or clothing) conceal a common spirituality. This is the prominent feature in Carroll's book and, even though we realize the obvious differences and distinctions between the two works, we will, nonetheless, attempt a connection. The aim is not to align the two works in order to explain the one with the other, but to provide two knots in our connective pattern that somehow drew together stories that belong to the different classifications of ethnography and fiction. The mirror, in this instance, is the object helping us walk our connecting line; the tool through which human imagination comes in touch with the enthralling multiplicity of human existence.

Fabulous monsters

Everything has the potential to appear human-like in *Alice Through the Looking-Glass*. Animals, inanimate objects, insects and plants not only behave like persons but also have different perspectives on reality. The White Queen explains to Alice that life, in her own perspective, goes backwards, and this is certainly for the best since memory can work both ways: the things she remembers best, the queen says, are the things that occurred the week after the next. A gnat the size of a chicken is having a perfectly normal discussion with Alice, suggesting that it's entirely pointless for insects to have a name if they won't answer to it. The first thing that Alice notices, once through the looking-glass, is that all sort of inanimate objects are being animated. The clock on the mantelpiece has the face of a smiling old man, while in the untidy atmosphere of the looking-glass room the chess-pieces are moving and talking to each other. In fact, they exist in pairs: The Red Queen and the Red King, the White Queen and the White King are sitting together on the shovel, chessmen are wandering about and two Castles are walking arm in arm. Amazingly, stepping through literatures' mirror, we do not find reflections but a trail to a non-anthropocentric understanding of the world similar to that of Amerindian perspectivism where different species experience different realities, but all share a common humanity. Alice does not simply enter that world; she engages into a dialogue with it.

Viveiros de Castro suggested that while multiculturalist cosmologies – Western cosmologies – are based on the idea of a unity of nature and a plurality of cultures (our bodies are the same but we have differences in spirit) for the Amerindian societies, we are spiritually the same but are different in physicality. This might mean that a human and an animal are equally a 'person' bearing inside the same humanity, while their bodies are different. Similarly, a human from a different tribe might not be considered to be a 'person' despite the obvious bodily similarities. Therefore, the term 'multinatural' (different physicalities) better fits the Amerindian perspective where culture is the guaranteed and the universal while physical substance is the particular. Similarly, whatever the physical form of the creatures Alice meets along her journey – plants, animals, things – they all seem to behave as persons. The Sheep, to take but one of them, that Alice encounters in a little shop is described as sitting in a chair, knitting. From time to time, and in a grandmother's fashion, the Sheep would glance at Alice through huge eyeglasses. Both Alice and the Sheep engage in a long conversation that makes very little sense since each character has their own single view of reality and use of English language: when Alice asks the Sheep for permission to look around, the Sheep points at the sheer impossibility of her request, as Alice may look in front of her and on both sides but never all around her – she clearly does not possess eyes at the back of her head. Trying to do as she is told, Alice looks at the shelves in order to find something to buy, but, keeping with the theme of animism, items are starting to move away from her. In the end, the incidence with the sheep becomes even more absurd: Alice finds herself inside a little boat gliding along a river, while the Sheep declares her to be a little goose.

This is how 'fictional perspectivism' is depicted in Carroll's story. But what happens when parallel qualities exist, not inside the pages of a book, but somewhere in our own very real world? How do humans and animals see themselves and each other in this case? According to Viveiros de Castro, humans view 'humans as humans, animals as animals and spirits (if they see them) as spirits; however, animals (predators) and spirits see humans as animals (as prey) to the same extent that animals (as prey) see humans as spirits or as animals (predators)'.[5] Animals, on the other hand, see themselves as humans. They think they are anthropomorphic creatures, living in human houses and participating in human cultural activities. They also believe that they are eating human food – Viveiros de Castro writes how blood may be perceived as beer by jaguars and maggots are believed to be fish by vultures.

What if Alice was there? An opening chapter of such a story could see Alice entering a village, full of palm trees, exotic birds and inhabited by jaguars. Alice could enter a hut, to find two jaguars that think they are sitting on a dinner table, talking about their day and drinking beer. Alice would see the jaguars as animals, and find their human behaviour and talking abilities very strange, while the jaguars would be astonished by Alice's presence, not being certain as to what kind of animal is she. Quite a similar incidence exists in *Alice Through the Looking-Glass*, when Alice meets a Lion and a Unicorn at war with each other. Both animals are pictured by Helen Oxenbury as standing on two feet, engaging in what appears to be a feast fight. When the Unicorn sees Alice he is shocked and appalled by her sight and demands to be told immediately what is this. When he is informed by Haigha – illustrated as a walking hare wearing white ballerina shoes, a robe and a brown bag hanging around his neck – that *this* is a human child, the Unicorn declares her to be a 'fabulous monster'. But then, he is curious to know if the child is alive. All that time, of course, Alice is referred to as 'it' by everyone in the company. Haigha then points out that Alice must be alive since she can talk. As a proof, Alice is asked to speak. Alice obliges, saying that she too thinks unicorns to be 'fabulous monsters' and that, so far, she had never seen one alive before. What the Unicorn replies is, perhaps, the ticket to understanding and appreciating any world which is different to our own: 'Well now that we *have seen* each other,' said the Unicorn, 'if you'll believe in me, I'll believe in you. Is that a bargain?'[6]

Alice's story also presents us with an essential discovery: to find ourselves in a remarkable world of endless possibility, we need a broken mirror. We need to allow the solid glass to disappear and come to terms with the fact that what we have been looking at in the mirror, all this time, is an illusion. We can of course choose to maintain that illusion, stay firm in front of the mirror's frame, or we can create a more flexible space where the glass used to stand. The second choice is more interesting. We call it the gaze of imagination: our mirror image, in this case, does not simply mimic and reflect us but may also – as in the case of Alice – change us, disagree with us, guide us into somewhere else.

Animals are people

While in Carroll's fiction animals appear to wear human clothes, or to walk with their hands in their pockets, in De Castro's ethnography, bodily characteristics like fur or claws are considered to be an external form. 'In sum, animals are people, or see themselves as persons ... the manifest form of each species is a mere envelope (a "clothing") which conceals an internal human form'.[7] Different physicality which would serve to differentiate the species, is indigenously perceived as clothes, particular skins that all enclose the same inner humanity. 'Thus, humanity is both a constant and a variable, a common interiority and a multi-form physicality. Every physicality is human physicality, but with some distinguishing diacritical marking.'[8] In Alice's world this is evident as all creatures, regardless of their skin or physical appearance, believe themselves to be human and behave as such. Even the Red Queen (an object) sees herself as a human queen and acts accordingly: in the beginning of the story, she declares that all ways in the world belong to her. In the looking-glass world, animals and objects are illustrated having their own distinct form while, most of the times, also bearing pieces of human clothing. Things, even though for the most part maintain their shapes, are often pictured with a human face: Humpty Dumpty is depicted in the form of an egg but still possesses eyes, ears, a nose, a mouth, hands and feet. In addition, he is wearing a cravat and becomes indeed very upset when Alice mistakes it for a belt. As Humpty Dumpty makes clear, his cravat is a present from the White King and Queen. A frog, later on in the story, appears before Alice dressed in bright yellow and wearing big boots.

For an Amazonian tribe, a Jaguar can be a person, and its claws are a distinctive feature, a natural accessory like gloves or a scarf. No matter the clothes, skin, or fur, humanity and not animality is the original stage for all species. This common and shared interiority that endures within many bodily forms often finds expression in the cosmogonic myths of the Amerindians. In some of them an explanation is offered on how animals once came to lose their human qualities. It goes like this: at first, animals and humans were persons, both had consciousness, language, and intentionality, but then animals changed and acquired more distinctive characteristics and places.

People did not change but continued to be human. Therefore, 'animals are ex-humans, not humans ex-animals.'[9] Applied to Alice's story, for instance, where she meets the knitting sheep, we would identify their encounter as belonging to a past time, where both humans and animals unfailingly shared common qualities and enjoyed a human interiority. If we were to continue in the spirit of the Amerindian myths, Alice would go on to behave like a human being, but the sheep who appeared dressed in human clothes, thinking and speaking, would change to assume different forms. In some of them it would continue to appear like a human-sheep, keeping a shop and rowing on boats, in others, it would perfectly resemble an animal-sheep. It might also inhabit different places: human places or spirit worlds.

Philippe Descola is another anthropologist studying societies where any clear distinction between humans and non-humans as we know it in the Western world does not exist.[10] Paying particular attention to the relations of native groups with their environment, Descola theorized on cosmologies in which spirits, animals or plants belong, along with humans, to the same category of 'persons'. Animism is one of the four modes of identification (i.e. the various properties of existing beings, human and non-human, as well as the ways of experiencing the world). The other three are defined as: totemism, naturalism and analogism.[11] Animism is presented as the main mode of identification among the hunters of Siberia, South and North America, and parts of Asia and Melanesia, where a marked similarity of interiority is perceived among a great variety of different species. Simply put, humans and non-human species have similar qualities and spirits but different bodies. In some occasions, this continuous interiority extends not only to animals but to plants as well, or even to physical phenomena and planets – the sun and moon, for example – regardless of the apparently different physicality between species, and between species and things. Humans, animals, plants, objects might be considered to be a person with thoughts, language and self-consciousness. Physical bodies exist in multi-forms, each with its own special ways of growth, reproduction and existence in a habitat, but their differentiation does not forbid species to be connected by a human interiority and even see themselves as having a human physicality in addition to their own. Therefore, different species have human physicality with distinctive features: people are humans-humans while vultures are vultures-humans and plants are plants-humans.

In Alice's world, characters have similar interiority but are different in appearance or physicality. Alice, for instance, is a human-human, while the Lion is a lion-human creature. And since each of those characters perceive and experience their being-in-the-world in a distinctive way (the Unicorn believes that Alice is a monster and that a cake should be handed around first and then cut in pieces), we might say that Alice's world is characteristic of perspectival animism: a world where Descola's animism and de Castro's perspectivism are in constant dialogue. So, far from encountering her self-reflection, Alice's journey takes an unexpected ontological turn: from a fantasy world of mirrors into an animistic reality, where all creatures and things share an underlying humanity but express multiple and incompatible points of view. The mirror's glass dissolved into a silver mist, allowing us to find the looking-glass world: a place that does not quite exist, but imitate, in the peculiar style of a mirroring, the ontology of another.

The gaze of imagination

Carroll's mirror is clearly misused. Alice looks into it with the eyes of a child. That means looking into the mirror to find not a face but an adventure. In this manner, her face, room and reality do not matter much – if at all. For Alice, existence is possible in the absence of interest in her own reflection. But what kind of existence becomes possible in the light of that loss? The answer lies in a series of overlapping but distinct lines of thinking. First of all, the mirror becomes an object of infinite possibilities: in collaboration with our imagination, it gives being to what does not exist. This should not be surprising. The mirror is an amazing object to imagine with. It takes us deep into envisioned settings but still reflects the rest of the world – in the case of Carroll's story, the rest of the drawing room – it still imposes a kind of order. The mirror, therefore, serves as a unique aid of human imagination in the sense of offering a space of absolute freedom while, by design, maintaining a basic framework of bendable reality.

Let us now, as a second step, concentrate on loss – the 'real' mirroring in the looking-glass we are willing to forfeit for the sake of an adventure. Do you remember the case of Carpenter and the feelings of tribal terror the mirror image provoked to the members of the Biami tribe? It is not unusual for the mirror to provoke contrasting emotions or to relate to opposing situations. Freud has commented that once he watched his grandson engaged in two games of loss: one as he looked himself in the mirror, and then as he crouched beneath its level. For Freud the experience was associated with the separation of a child from its mother.[12] Jacques Lacan claimed that human beings are not born having the capacity to understand their separation with their environment and the world.[13] This skill is acquired with the help of mirror gazing during the time he called 'the mirror stage' where an infant is starting to recognize its mirrored image. According to Lacan, the mirror stage comes between the ages of eight to eighteen months. Learning to recognize ourselves in the mirror and internalizing our mirror reflection creates a concrete body image and helps us locate ourselves in space. By the end of the mirror stage, humans obtain 'the armour of an alienating identity'.[14] Recognizing itself in the mirror, the child now identifies with its external image and in doing so 'it shifts from the illusion of oneness (identity with the caregiver and the image in the mirror) to the inevitability of separation'.[15]

The loss of togetherness, the process of alienation that begins with mirror self-recognition, results in an 'outside' world which is differentiated from us: self and others acquire thick impenetrable borders. Inevitably, the sense of being united with the rest of the world is lost. We are becoming individuals, as if by force. What do we gain? Eventually, we assume our personal identities. We come to know who we are and, because of the mirror, what do we look like to others. There is only one point in Carroll's story when that acquired identity is lost: the moment when Alice enters the wood with no names. Keeping with the theme of disorientation, and on her way to the Eighth Square, Alice enters this dark forest where all things are nameless. Once in there Alice forgets her own name, as well as the names of the trees, the flowers, the birds and everything else in that forest. Alice realizes what is happening – she was prepared for it – and is determined to recall her name. She fails. All she can wrongly assume now is that her name begins with an 'L'.

It is at that time of confusion and identity loss that a fawn comes her way. The fawn seems unaware of its name too and feels no fear of Alice's presence. And for as long as neither human nor animal have any idea who they are, they walk together with Alice putting her arms tenderly around the neck of the fawn. At that point any sense of mirroring in Alice's story completely vanishes, along with her sense of self. Because of that loss, Alice, through a broken mirror, becomes one with the forest and its creatures. Nameless and, in a way, selfless, they keep going peacefully in each other's company. But as soon as they get further away, the fawn remembers it is a fawn and recognizes Alice as a human child. The strangely harmonious and almost mystical atmosphere is vanished. The fawn cries out their separate identities and is suddenly terrified of Alice. In a state of alarm, the animal dashes away, leaving behind a saddened Alice on the verge of tears. That was the one short point in the book where Alice appeared to be in harmony with a creature of the looking-glass world, for otherwise, they all seemed weird and funny and sometimes even scary and frustrating. In this short scene, the eternal crisis of separation and individuation is nicely exemplified. Out of the woods, Alice and the fawn possess a new knowledge – the knowledge of the self – possible mainly through the mirror image. Both, in a way, suddenly 'wear' Lacan's armour of alienating identity. The sense of a united universe is now unattainable.

Broken mirror

In front of the mirror we are presented with a view that exceeds our natural capacity of vision. We gaze at an image which, first of all, includes us as an object in full form. We also gaze at the world as if we have eyes on our back. But there is always a blind spot. Alice notices that spot – the place behind the fireplace – and builds an alternative universe based on that curiosity. Thus, linking knowledge and imagination, she constructs a world that is not only beyond her vision but also beyond existence. For the construction of that universe, the mirror provides the scaffolding. For our mirror-gazing exercise, in this chapter, we attempt to do the same. That is, we look in the mirror not to find our self-reflection but a world around it, and beyond it; we step through the looking-glass ourselves.

The aim is to break our habitual interaction with the mirror. To experience how it feels like when we are not concerned with our looks and to explore in what ways this is possible. Hopefully, looking *through* the mirror and not *at* it, we will achieve, at least for a short moment, a creative gaze: the kind that imagines universes beyond reflection.

This way of looking in the mirror is defined by unguarded expectation and is open to multiple interpretations of the world. It is also gullible; it begs for surprises, it creates drama. How we appear on the glass is not part of this story. The narrative produced by the mirror will be of things we take very little notice of – like that space behind the fireplace. The exciting question is thus: what else is there?

To think this way about the mirror is to begin to work out what it reflects not as a readymade image but as a site of aesthetic traces, signs and material memories. Timothy Morton calls it, 'an object-oriented view of causality'.[16] In that sense, the mirror image is like performance art. A reflective surface where you can choose and construct a personal, undisciplined reality. The mirror will do for us what it does for every writer: it will give us a frame to create a story. It will present us, automatically, with a phantom of our material surroundings. It is up to us to envision possible extensions: worlds related to but are not in accordance with our own. So, apart from us, what else appears in the looking-glass? If there is a door where does that door open to? If there is a wall what might be behind it?

In a way, this is an exercise of neglect. We ignore our mirror image; we pass over it in search of creative and imaginary narratives and alternate mode of existence. This is not how things should be. Mirrors are not there for us to exercise our creativity. They are there to help us see our body. Society is also there to force us to put judgement on what we see. Still, pondering in front of the mirror on the idea of a world beyond, one may find extraordinary things. Alice did find a looking-glass world. We could outline our own, or even come to terms with our unwillingness to do so. Perhaps we feel more comfortable with a world that revolves around and ends firmly on our mirrored self. After all, the gaze of imagination cannot offer a full view, but only ephemeral glimpses of a world that would be confusing and unreliable: a world we can enter briefly, and completely alone.

There is always a choice. In case we choose to look *through* the mirror and not *at* it, we might even find a world without reflections: a world of 'togetherness', of less rigid selves where we do not know our names or do not care to remember them. The 'armour of alienating identity' might fall off our shoulders. Like Alice, we may walk into a forest where all beings are united. Behind the blind spot of our mirror is where our own deer appears. First, it approaches a river. It leans its head over the water. No reflection of its face. It looks closer. Again, no mirroring. The deer stares at us in surprise, with its large brown eyes. Then, it walks close to us, swiftly and hurriedly as if it has been waiting for this moment for years and, for the first time, touches us with its head. We suddenly understand what the deer is saying to us. We realize that, all this while, we have been sharing the same household. We touch each other to keep warm. We can keep it that way, as long as we stand in front of the mirror and see no face in it. But how long can that be?

The other in the mirror

Masters and slaves

What we see in the mirror might not always be our choice. Sometimes, the mirror presents us with a strange face – a face which is not our own – even when we do not cast in it an adventurous gaze. Other times, and even as the mirror reflects our face faithfully, it nevertheless leaves us with a peculiar sense of doubt: 'is it really me?' It is almost as if the mirror has a choice on how to reflect us. What do we mean? We will spend this chapter explaining.

Let's begin where Lewis Carroll's *Alice Through the Looking-Glass* ends: that is the point where Alice wakes up.[1] There, it becomes obvious that Carroll's imagined universe was one of dreams. The threat usually entailed in a strange world inside a mirror is absent. The atmosphere is light-hearted, full of puns and jokes, and there is only one point where things take a more sinister turn: the dream of the Red King hypothesis. In Chapter 4, Tweedledum and Tweedledee challenge Alice to think about the possibility of her being, not real, but a character in the king's dream. The Red King, in the meantime, is sleeping in the woods, snoring wildly and piercingly. Alice, who at first thinks she is listening to the roar of a beast, objects strenuously to the idea of being part of the king's sleep – a king who does not even look like one at all, collapsed on the grass with his red sleeping gown and night cap. As Tweedledum and Tweedledee insist that Alice does not really exist and will vanish when the king wakes up, the girl starts to cry. Alice certainly gets lost several times, faces criticism by unfamiliar creatures and encounters a fair amount of nonsense in the duration of her adventure, but this is the only time when doubt is cast over her survival. Of course, being present in a looking-glass world entails a risk on one's existence. Appearing might not mean living, but being a living image, a mirror phantom, a ghost. Still, this passing suggestion does not alter the playful impression of Alice's looking-glass world into something ominous. If we would like to examine a more perilous mirror world then, perhaps, writer, essayist and poet Jorge Luis Borges' gaze would fit us best.

In his story 'Fauna of Mirrors', Borges' imagination takes us back to the times of the Yellow Emperor: an era where both worlds, the specular and the human, are inhabited by people.[2] Passing through mirrors and crossing the border of these worlds is not something extraordinary. On the contrary, human people and mirror people are in regular contact and living in harmony with one another – even though the mirror people are different, and their world inside the mirror is nothing like our own in shapes and in colours. But then, the mirror people invade the earth and war breaks. Humans win the bloody feud because of the powerful magic of the Yellow Emperor. The mirror people are sentenced to act as humans' mirror images, up to this very day. So, what we actually see when we look in the mirror is not our double, but our mimic-slave. Deprived of their powers and their own forms, the mirror people are there to endlessly serve us. A world of warning: Borges ends his tale with the grim prophecy of a second war between the specular and the human realm. The Emperor's spell, he writes, is not going to last forever. The mirror creatures will eventually awaken. First, the Fish will start to stir in the mirror's depth and a line in a colour unseen before by any human will finally become visible. Then, gradually, the mirror people will start to disobey us, to move differently than us and reclaim their own forms. Once free from iron or glass, the mirror people will attack and, this time, will win the compact. A clatter of weapons, the writer tells us, coming from the depths of our mirrors, will signal the new war.

Borges has always been afraid of the looking-glass. His poem *Mirrors* starts with this very confession: the horror the writer feels in the presence of a mirror. The sense that, within the four walls of a room the 'crystal spies on us'.[3] Borges' imaginary gaze casts light onto the endless tension between body and reflection, person and mirrored self. In his writing, a mirror in a room disrupts one's loneliness and invades one's privacy. It is no wonder, then, that through Borges' mirror gaze our reflection, 'the other in the mirror', becomes our enemy; a prisoner of war chained down and forced into mimesis by a powerful spell. Borges also raises an interesting point: being a mirror image is a life sentence;

to mimic something is to be its slave. Perhaps this is something to consider as we try to mimic the images from advertising and fashion industry. There is also something else: Borges claims that we've won the war. We are the masters of our reflection. Indeed, our reflection unfailingly imitates our movement in the mirror. On the other hand, we depend on it for self-awareness. From our mirroring we seek knowledge of who we are, of how other people see us, in short, our thoughts and behaviour are guided by a slavish, immaterial mirror phantom; so what does that make us? Can it be the case that, concerning our mirroring, we are simultaneously masters and slaves?

At least in one thing, Borges is right: it is not over. Nothing is ever done with when it comes to one's mirror reflection. Understanding it, putting it into words is, by all means, a constant struggle. As self-image has taken on a tremendous significance, the mirror seems to occupy more and more of our thoughts. Even without the second war of Borges' prophecy, and without the clatter of any weapons, the mirror people are gaining ground.

Mirror fiction

The mirror is a curious object. If we do not look in it we lose, at least partly, our sense of self. If we do look, we might become trapped and victimized. The knowledge acquired through the mirror is, therefore, never easy. It is an unsettling form of knowledge, pricy and full of thorns, and it comes with the introduction of a specular double – a phantom-self which appears at an outside, alienating space. Now, if we are to stare in the mirror, continuously and with guided determination, something unexpected might happen. At this time, we refer to a series of experiments done by the psychologist Giovanni Caputo. The experiments included the witnessing of strange faces in the mirror by people gazing at their reflected image in a dimly lit room.[4] The basic experimental design was simple. In a quiet room, lit by a 25W light placed on the floor behind the participant observers so as not to be visible, a big mirror was placed in front of the observer's face at a 0.4-metre distance. Fifty healthy, young individuals were involved in the study. The task was to stare for ten minutes at their mirrored faces. As Caputo reports, it took less than a minute for them to perceive what he called 'the strange face illusion'.

That is, an unfamiliar face, staring back at them inside the mirror. When the ten-minute mirror gazing session ended, all the participants reported striking deformation of their mirror reflection. Their description of what they saw in the mirror varied from person to person including considerable deformation of their own faces, an unknown face, a parent's face either alive or deceased, the face of an animal, imaginary monsters and lastly some of the participants reported witnessing archetypal faces or ancestral portraits in the mirror (an old woman, a shaman, a child).

In simple words, the familiar mirror faces of the participants disappeared. Strange ones, other people's faces – both living and dead – animal faces like cats, pigs or lions, even fantastical monstrous beings appeared inside the looking-glass. Those new mirror faces, Caputo writes, produced to the participants a sensation of otherness, a kind of a dissociative identity effect. Anxiety was reported by participants who perceived a malign expression on the strange mirror face. Positive emotions, on the other hand, were experienced when the face in the mirror appeared to be smiling or cheerful. The vision of monstrous beings in the mirror – like a witch or a skull – produced mainly fear and uneasiness. Dead relatives were associated with pensive emotions and a contemplative mood. Caputo reports that, overall, the experiment evoked intense emotional reactions and was, at times, an unsettling experience.

The 'others' that people see in the mirror under those circumstances are, of course, not really there. Images conjured up inside one's mind – a haphazard mix of local and global facial features, phantoms of one's peripheral vision, emotions and memories – are all coming together to produce visions and images that have nothing to envy of Borges' fantasy. So what do we learn? First of all, a scientific fact: visual illusions, that is, the perception of strange looking-glass faces, can easily be witnessed by subjects during a lab experiment. There is indeed a mirror gaze capable to summon something as extraordinary as monsters and witches. Finally, the mirror is not to be trusted – that last part, of course, we already knew. Yet, we are prone to believe the mirror's fiction. Partly because our behaviour in front of the mirror, and the things we see in it, is seldom deprived of meaning. Strange-face illusions may be the psychodynamic projection of the subject's unconscious archetypal contents into the mirror image. Therefore, strange-face illusions might provide both an ecological setting and an experimental technique for the 'imaging of the unconscious.'[5]

To put it simply, what we see in the mirror is not really there, but it might well be in our minds. The strange images we stare at inside the looking-glass, Caputo claims, may be projected by us as part of our unconscious. Open to challenges, the validity of this claim is subject to further research. Nevertheless, Caputo, influenced by Jung's ideas on psychology and alchemy, claims a possible connection between archetypal contents and strange-face illusion. Among others, he refers to the archetype of the shadow in connection to the strange-face illusions of witches and monsters perceived by naive observers. He also refers to the strange-face illusion of the old man in relation to the archetype of the old sage. Strange-face illusions, different from pseudo-hallucinations produced by magic mirrors, are, according to Caputo, more likely to reflect the projection of archetypes.

While real mirrors are tools of self-awareness and, possibly, surfaces for the projection of the unconscious, literary mirrors are there to accommodate myriads of possibilities. Unrestricted, the literary mirror can summon into being any image conceivable. In other words, the 'other' in the mirror can take any form.

Erised

We start with the description of a famous mirror hidden away in the magical Hogwarts Castle. In J. K. Rowling's '*Harry Potter and the Philosopher's Stone*', a young wizard named Harry, wandering illicitly in the library's restricted section, enters an empty classroom in order to escape Argus Filch, the school's caretaker.[6] Once in there, his attention is caught by an object standing out among piled desks and chairs: 'something that didn't look as if it belonged there, something that looked as if someone had just put it there to keep it out of the way. It was a magnificent mirror, as high as the ceiling, with an ornate gold frame, standing on two clawed feet.'[7] Upon its frame the phrase 'Erised stra ehru oyt ube cafru oyt on wohsi' was inscribed. A phrase which, at first glance, means nothing, but spelled backwards as if reflected in a mirror, it reads: 'I show not your face but your heart's desire'. In a similar manner – the manner of the reverse printing of the *Jabberwocky*, the looking-glass poetry book – the name of the mirror 'Erised' actually reads 'desire'.

Thus, facing Harry Potter inside the dimly lit classroom is the ancient mirror of desire, that is not there for self-reflection.

Being true to its promise the mirror presents Harry Potter, once he steps in front of it, with a totally unexpected image: he is now surrounded by other people. 'He had to clap his hands to his mouth to stop himself screaming. He whirled around ... for he had seen not only himself in the mirror but a whole crowd of people standing right behind him.'[8] Petrified, Harry checks over his shoulder, only to realize that no one seems to be standing there; the room is deserted and silent. Looking into the mirror again, however, the mysterious crowd reappears right behind him. At first, the startled boy thinks that the people he sees might be invisible to the naked eye and only the mirror can reveal them. But as his repeated attempts to touch them fail, Harry Potter realizes that the weird crowd exists only inside the glass. The woman standing closer to him, crying and smiling at the same time, Harry believes to be his mother.

> A woman standing right behind his reflection was smiling at him and waving ... She had dark red hair and her eyes – her eyes are just as mine, Harry thought ... The tall, thin, black-haired man standing next to her put his arms around her. He wore glasses, and his hair was untidy. It stuck up at the back, just like Harry's did.[9]

Soon, it becomes clear that Harry is staring at his parents and other family members. 'Harry was so close to the mirror now that his nose was nearly touching that of his reflection. "Mum?" he whispered. "Dad?"'[10] Only his parents were dead.

If we were to make a comparison, we could say that the 'strange face in the mirror', in the case of Rowling's novel, takes the form of dead relatives. In a way, Harry Potter's mirror gazing meets Caputo's criteria: the room as described by the writer is only half-lit and Harry Potter is staring continuously in the looking-glass. Many of Caputo's subjects did claim to see faces of dead parents in the mirror. The faces provoked intense emotional reactions and pensive feelings – a dead parent looking at you from the depth of the looking-glass is bound to be mesmerizing and eerie. Yet, the fictional boy who stares in the mirror is experiencing, we learn from Dumbledore, the effects of magic: inside the mirror of Erised the faces of the dead do not just appear staring – they move, smile and wave. 'Harry looked into the faces of the other people and saw other pairs of green eyes like his, even a little old man who looked as though he had Harry's knobbly knees … The Potters smiled and waved at Harry and he stared hungrily back at them, his hands pressed flat against the glass as though he was hoping to fall right through and reach them.'[11] Imagination augments the mirror's natural capacities to surprise and enchant us: it enhances the mirror's enticing qualities; it builds upon them. An original uncanny trick, the mirror's attraction for images and apparitions that are not 'us', becomes the core around which fantastical stories and fictional universes are built. The mirror of Erised reflects the deepest desire of everyone that stands in front of it. It turns desire to vision and thus captivates its victims.

Rowling's story does a great job weaving together wish and self-reflection, anchoring the relationship in the material object of the mirror. The desire of the mirror of Erised – desire spelled backwards – can bring madness just as easily as it can bring delight. In fact, the mirror is cruel. The desire it brings forth is, in the words of Dumbledore, a desperate one: 'It shows us nothing more or less than the deepest, most desperate desire of our hearts.'[12] But it is a desire of fundamental lack: the mirror gives to the viewer a visual taste of their obsessions. The vision can be maintained for as long as one remains fixed in front of it. Like all mirrors, the mirror of Erised is in its unique way a perfect trap. It captures the observer using as bait a dominant, fixating longing.

Rowling points to an all too human characteristic: the chase of the impossible self in front of the looking-glass. In the case of Harry Potter, that impossible self takes the form of a boy surrounded by parents and a loving extended family; a boy who is no longer an orphan. The magic mirror in Rowling's writing produces a destructive gaze that triggers and aggravates feelings of need and dissatisfaction. It is a gaze that begs for whatever we have not. Without offering guidance or opportunity, the mirror of Erised provides us with glimpses at an unattainable, idolized existence – an 'if only' that suddenly becomes agonizingly visible.

A portrait's gaze

Dorian Grey, the young, handsome aristocrat in Oscar Wilde's *The Picture of Dorian Grey*, has his portrait painted by his friend and artist Basil Hallward.[13] Infatuated by his own beauty, Dorian Grey becomes desperate at the idea of ageing, while his portrait remains unaltered and eternally beautiful. He becomes envious of his portrait and a terrible wish takes form: Dorian Grey declares he is ready to give up his soul for the situation to be reversed. That is, for the portrait to age while he remains forever young. The living subject, in other words, becomes jealous of the image's still nature and wishes it upon himself. At the same time, the image acquires the human ability of transformation. That the transformation is horrific has to do with the moral of the story: sin comes at a dire cost.

So, the portrait of Dorian Grey becomes an image that shares life experience with its subject. The despair of Dorian Grey over old age and the fading of youth bring about the 'humanization' of his picture, which in itself leads up to the abolishment of a great divide: that between human and painted image. The extraordinary eradication of that boundary results in a catastrophic disembodiment of experience: Dorian acts upon the world but remains untouched by it. The world cannot act upon Dorian. Time and action is to be marked only on his image: it is the face of his portrait that is tainted by Dorian's very first act of cruelty. The night he abandons Sibyl Vane, the innocent young actress he used to love, his deed becomes evident not on his face but on canvas. That night, after watching her giving a talentless performance, Dorian is told by Sibyl that she is quitting the stage. The young girl is not interested in acting anymore. She plans to devote her life entirely to him. But Dorian loved Sibyl the brilliant actress. Disappointed, he tells her that without her acting, she is of no interest to him. He tells her that she has failed him and heartlessly leaves her sobbing and crouching on the floor.

On his return home, Dorian notices that his portrait has changed. The expression on the face seems altered as if his lips are now touched by cruelty. Utterly surprised, Dorian draws up the blind in the hope that the impression of callousness would be swept away from his picture, along with all other fantastic shadows that have taken shelter into the dimness of his room. He looks again. Yet, the light of dawn makes the change even more noticeable. 'The quivering, ardent sunlight showed him the lines of cruelty round the mouth as clearly as if he had been looking into a mirror after he had done some dreadful thing.'[14] This is the first time in Oscar Wilde's story that Dorian's picture acts as a mirror of a very specific sort: a mirror that reveals to Dorian not the reflection of his face but what his face would have looked like if it still had the capacity to register the life of its owner. Indeed, that capacity had now passed over to the painting and Dorian's skin was never to alter again in any way. Unlike any human being, his flesh is not accountable to his deeds. His image, on the other hand, would bear the burns of his excesses.

In the beginning the young man is content by his new reality. If anything, he feels sorry for his painted image, for it would have to suffer the scars and blows of time and of his sins. The image will reflect Dorian's life, and Dorian will have to gaze at it, as one gazes upon one's mirror for self-awareness. The image, in other words, is to become responsive to Dorian's life in ways that Dorian himself will never be. Thus, Dorian becomes a soulless spectator of his actions. He declares his portrait to be 'the most magical of mirrors',[15] revealing his soul to him and having access on secrets about his life that he himself has not: 'It (the portrait) had received the news of Sibyl Vane's death before he had known of it himself. It was conscious of the events of life as they occurred. The vicious cruelty that marred the fine lines of the mouth had, no doubt, appeared at the very moment that the girl had drunk the poison.'[16]

A new and more powerful narrator has emerged to take over Dorian's story. Dorian has forfeited this role. The reciprocal interaction between body and world is not evident on his skin, and thus, his mirrored self is deprived of stories. There is a profound emptiness and boredom involved in Dorian's eternal youth. So much so that in the end Dorian, for all his beauty, becomes disenchanted by it. The story of his life, his passions, his secrets, his triumphs or failures, are all to be told by a picture. Dorian becomes aware that his relationship with the looking-glass is now obsolete. The line of cruelty around his lips that Dorian noticed on his portrait are absent in the mirror and so will be all other marks. 'He winced, and, taking up from the table an oval glass framed in ivory Cupids, one of Lord Henry's many presents to him, glanced hurriedly into its polished depths. No line like that warped his red lips. What did it mean?'[17] It means that from then on, mirrors in the story of Dorian Grey are the most useless of objects. The only true mirror is the portrait and the only gaze that matters is the portrait's gaze. Through the portrait's eyes Dorian's disintegrated soul is looking straight at him – burdened first with the terrible gravity of Sibyl Vane's suicide and later on with Hallward's murder. It is indeed a terrifying gaze and it makes Dorian, for all his beauty, conscious of himself as a dreadful object to behold.

Almost two decades later, Dorian stares in that same mirror Lord Henry has given him. This time, Dorian is very much aware of the 'still' nature of his mirroring. His eternal youth has lost its appeal; his unstained beauty now seems more like sarcasm. Once again, the mirror that Oscar Wilde interestingly describes as a 'polish shield',[18] reflects Dorian's unsullied appearance. Enraged, Dorian thinks that the mirror reveals nothing of him but a fake facade that conceals his true identity. His face is indeed there on the glass but it is not him: his true, disfigured and hideous self is staring at him from the hidden portrait. For Dorian Grey the 'other in the mirror' is a living mask – a vision of eternal youth, pinned down against the currents of time like a dead butterfly. 'His beauty has been to him but a mask, his youth but a mockery.'[19] The mirror image has taken the qualities of a painting: a frozen past moment forever extending into the present. A dismayed Dorian throws the mirror on the floor and manically crashes it into splinters. The destruction of the mirror is a crucial moment in the story and the dire consequence to follow is, perhaps, the reason that Oscar Wilde called it 'a shield' in the first place.[20] The symbolic death of the mirror now leaves Dorian 'shield-less' at the mercy of his portrait. The portrait's gaze, unopposed by Dorian's gaze in the looking-glass, splits Dorian in two: his body becomes a timeless alien while his soul and conscience relocate on the canvas. At the same time, the portrait feels like a stranger to Dorian – an appalling stranger, reproaching and punishing him ceaselessly for his moral faults. The portrait, now, instead of a magical mirror becomes 'an unjust mirror, this mirror of his soul that he was looking at.'[21]

Jacques Lacan's distinction between eye and gaze finds distinct parallel in the story of Dorian Grey.[22] Dorian becomes painfully aware of his body as both, subject and object, the seeing and the seen. In a reversibility of vision, the man's face is now looked at critically by his portrait. In fact, the human eye – Dorian's eye gazing in the mirror – becomes irrelevant but the portrait's gaze strikes Dorian with a tyrannical, unbearable force, objectifying him in front of his own image. As a man untouched by life, Dorian is very hard to define. A different body exists for him in extracorporeal space and both 'bodies' – portrait and living Dorian – are reciprocally gazing at each other.

The gaze of the portrait verifies the loss of Dorian's innocence, the abolition of his humanity and inevitably his death. Dorian, unable to withstand the view of his picture, stubs it with the same knife he used to kill Basil Hallward years ago. But, by piercing the canvas, Dorian himself dies, assuming the form of a grotesque old man. The portrait now resembles a perfect young Dorian. Order between subject and object, lifeless reflection and living body, is restored and by Dorian's death the mirror is resurrected: the mirroring of Dorian's dead body would be that of an aged disfigured man.

Living masks

Let's continue with the theme of not recognizing or agreeing with what we see in the mirror. We have already discussed Caputo's mirror-gazing experiments that involved apparitions of strange faces in the mirror. Now, we will look into a related study by the same author, where subjects are staring into a mirror while wearing a mask. The aim of the experiments is to test whether individuals would experience the 'living mask illusion'. That is whether they would attribute living characteristic to an inanimate, human-like mask.[23] The mask in question is an original Japanese ritual mask – a Shinto mask of god Bugaku measuring 0.24 metre in width and 0.3 metre in height. Seven participants – four men and three women – wearing the mask were placed in a white 3 metre by 4 metre room under dim lighting and engaged in mirror gazing. The observers were unaware of the experiment's objective and, according to Caputo's report, all 'quite spontaneously described the worn mask as a living being, having living expressions, even if they had not been told this may happen in the initial instructions'.[24]

The mask-wearing observers stared at their self-reflection in a mirror measuring 0.5 metre by 0.5 metre. The mirror was placed on a tripod in the centre of the room and at a distance of 0.4 metre from the observers. The individuals were instructed to keep staring into the eyes of the mask, press the button in case the mask appeared to be alive and hold it for as long as the illusion was maintained. After a ten-minute mirror-gazing session, participants were asked to describe their experience. The experiment resulted in all mask-wearing participants perceiving apparitions of the living mask.

Classification of phenomenological descriptions, Caputo writes, demonstrates that the mask-wearing observers perceived apparitions of deformed traits, animals and monstrous beings. In relation to the previous mirror-gazing experiments, Caputo states that living masks and strange faces in the mirror are similar phenomena. Still, in the mask-wearing gazing sessions, all of the observers reported archetypal apparitions which involved a man (a serious man, a bearded man and a very old man), a smiling child, an ancient warrior, a Gorgon's head and a shaman. Caputo attributes the polymorphic apparitions to the evocative power of the Shinto mask. 'When a mask is worn, it temporarily turns into an embodied part of one's self or, in other words, the self is projected into a physical object, the mask, that is afforded into one's body neighbourhood.'[25] It is interesting that Dorian Grey, looking into the mirror for the last time in his life, claims he sees a mask: a beautiful young face staring back at him. Sensing the weight of his invisible years on his soul, he disowns the sight. Dorian Grey's beautiful, living face feels like a mask. In Caputo's experiment, on the other hand, the mask seems like a living face in the mirror.

The magic of eternal youth and the fear of growing old are two of the most compelling themes related to the mirror, either real or fictional. And for all its trickery, the mirror sustains its reputation as a precise and impartial judge of people's looks. In Sylvia Plath's poetry, for instance, the mirror even speaks to the reader in the first person, claiming to always be truthful and to reflect things just as they are.[26] Then, having no false modesty, the mirror declares itself to be the eye of a four-cornered god, uninfluenced by emotions. Nevertheless, the mirror is proved to be a liar because of a woman's gaze. That is, a woman who stares in it every day, searching for who she is.[27] The mirror claims to be faithful to the woman by reflecting justly everything it sees, but the woman, rewards its honesty with tears.[28] Obviously, the woman is not happy with what she sees.

But what does the woman see?

What is that truthful mirror image which, in the end, drives her to tears? The mirror claims to be looked at as if it was a lake. Bending over it every day, the woman is witnessing a little girl drowning, while the image of an old woman reaches towards her, resembling a horrifying fish. These are, in this case, the two 'others' in Plath's mirror. At this point, we realize that mirror images might not be so factual after all. At least, not in the eye of the observer. What we learn from the mirror's narrative has nothing to do with the woman's physical appearance – the colour of her eyes, the shape of her face, the curves of her lips. Instead of receiving the precise and clear mirror image we were promised at the beginning of the poem, we only get a sense of the woman's age – nothing specific, just that she is not at the blossom of her youth or at least she does not think that she is – and that she dreads growing old. The atmosphere is ominous and disturbing, owing to the imagery of the drowned girl (probably representing the loss of youth) and of the terrible fish that rises from the 'lake's' depths (which hints at the woman's idea of her future as an old person).

Like Dorian Grey, the lady in Plath's poem is horrified of future old age and desperate of losing, or having lost, her youth. She casts in her mirror a gaze so full of melancholy and fear that it clouds anything else we, or she, might have learnt from it. Even though, unlike Dorian Grey, her face is not frozen but changes with time, she is also in agony. To her, the ageing face is interpreted as the drowning of youth. To Dorian the youthful, unchanging face in the mirror is interpreted as a treacherous living mask. Both have one thing in common: they are disgusted by their mirroring. It seems that one can never get it right – concerning the mirrored self something will always be amiss.

Is it the mirror's fault? In Sylvia Plath's poem the mirror does its part. It reflects the woman faithfully, it follows her around the room, it 'clings' onto her. But the woman, as most people, does not simply accept her reflection. Instead, she interprets it. As a result, the exactness the mirror claims to offer in the beginning of the poem, the truthful reflection, becomes deeply subjective. 'The other in the mirror' becomes, once more, the enemy. Perhaps, by speaking directly to us, Sylvia Plath's mirror tries to communicate how poorly we are at interpreting our mirrored selves: 'I am impartial and precise. You just don't know how to look in me.'

This cannot be me

So, how do mirrors 'reflect' our imagination? In literature, mirrors reveal our deepest fears and wishes. Sometimes, even in real life they have the capacity to trick our gaze into seeing things that are not really there. Mirrors represent our worries and pleasures in various ways. Not all of us, for instance, associate growing up with imagery of dreadful fishes or are ready to bargain our soul to retain our youthful looks. Yet, to all of us, the self-reflection holds a specific importance. The mirror image 'touches' us in a way that no other image ever could: we do not look at our mirrored self like we do at anything else we see in front of us. We are immediately involved, mentally and physically. We are concerned. The relation of mirror and imagination is just as extraordinary. That is because the mirror 'agrees' with our imagination more than any other object: in fiction, pumpkins are turned into carriages and brooms fly, but there is no way that our broom would actually fly. A broom would never entertain or partake in our imaginings. The mirror is a different story. The mirror has a special affinity with fantasy. Gazing in it, the mirror evokes imaginary things into being. Harry Potter saw images of his dead parents in his magical mirror but there is a good chance that we can too, if, of course, we follow closely the instruction of Caputo's mirror-gazing experiments. For mirrors, fiction is not the opposite of reality. Reality and fiction blend. Daydreaming and desire, nightmares and subconscious fears are drawn into the looking-glass. This is not accidental. As Caputo's experiments demonstrate, the apparition of dead parents in the mirror may happen not only to fictional characters but to real observers under specific circumstances. Masks may come to life, animals and fantastical monsters may appear instead of one's face in the mirror. And what we learn is this: to the sentiment of not looking like ourselves in the mirror, to the odd 'this cannot be me' moment, the mirror fully agrees. If we search for others in the mirror, the mirror will oblige. For it is in its nature to create visual illusions, fictional selves, dissociative others. It is as if, unlike any other object, the mirror imagines together with its observer. It becomes an active conspirator in the creation of fantastical visions. In this way the mirror adds to the meaning and enigma of the reflected face.

We propose a mirror-gazing experiment to see if we can assume a new and unexpected self-reflection. In other words, to take the feeling of 'I am not looking quite myself today' and take it further. We suggest standing in a dimly lit and quiet room and gaze in the mirror without interruption for ten minutes. This is an exercise on the mysteries of the self: we test if it can 'slip away'. And if we see a strange face in the mirror, what would it look like? Would there be anything on it that we can still call our own? Of course, we may not even see a human face. There might be an imaginary creature or an animal. The very deer which took residence in this book waits for us, as the 'other' in our mirror. It seems inexplicable to be reflected there. It makes no sense. But it is not sense or the substantiality of one's face we are now seeking to explore in the mirror: it is its elusive nature. In fact, what we aim to realize is that hypnotically staring in the mirror is not the secret to finding who we are. Sometimes, even in a real mirror, reality is missing. Indeed, as the mirror has a very strange sense of humour, staring in it might result in an experience quite opposite to self-knowledge: a vision of Sylvia Path's terrible fish or Caputo's ghosts. The mirror is not always an objective space.

Yes, the mirror can speak the truth, but it can also devour it.

The gaze of the shaman

Mongolia: A land of permeable borders

Do people always look in the mirror? It may come as a surprise but, in some places of the world, the answer is no. But mirrors are there to be looked at, are they not? It depends. The mirror we are mostly familiar with is an object used and appreciated for its ability to reflect things. And yet, a different kind of mirror does exist – one which is valued for what lies beyond its non-reflective side. To find out more about this peculiar type of mirror, in this chapter, we follow the anthropologist Caroline Humphrey to North West and Easter Inner Mongolia and Buryatia.[1] Humphrey describes two kinds of mirrors: the household mirror (that has glass on one of its sides) and the shamanic mirror (usually made entirely out of brass or bronze). We begin with the former.

The household mirrors are massive and square. We find them opposite the door of the Mongol tent, in the *hoimor* (honourable place), positioned above a painted wooden chest (called the *avdvar*) that contains precious household belongings. Household mirrors never stand alone. They are surrounded by religious icons, pictures of family members, offerings and other valuable objects.

According to the anthropologist Rebecca Empson, young daughters-in-law or elderly female members of the family feed the Mongolian chest (*avdvar*) 'with offerings and attend to and change its form. In turn, visitors to a household are expected to respond to it. As one enters a house, after greeting the host, one is expected to go to the chest and, while bowing down towards it, knock one's head (*mörgöx*) against its surface three times and turn a prayer wheel or offer some money or sweets to the religious icons or to a portrait of the host's deceased relative.'[2]

The bulky mirror in the centre of the visual display in the *hoimor* is among the first things that one notices on entering the tent as it stands at its sacred place, the edge of the living space – behind it is outside. The mirror is heavily tilted and therefore hardly able to offer a reflection.[3] At times, the mirror is even turned around, with its shiny surface facing the wall like a naughty child or covered completely with a cloth. Clearly, our familiar practice of self-inspection cannot account for the Mongolian household mirror.

So what does the mirror do?

According to Humphrey, the mirrors are possibly put on houses for their luminosity and multiplicity effects. They are used for lighting up the space and enriching and doubling the surrounding precious objects. But mirrors have also hidden and dangerous qualities. Buryats of Eastern Mongolia fret that mirrors absorb and reproduce appalling events: an upsetting quarrel, a death in the family, a thunder storm can be taken in by the mirror and leaked out at any time in the future with unpredicted consequences. That is why, when such events occur, mirrors should be concealed, turned around or covered up completely.

Reflections of things happened may reside inside a mirror.[4] A household mirror, therefore, is full of family secrets. It contains stories, shadows and images of the past (good or bad), that should never be out in public. So, mirrors are not to be sold. Rather, they have to be destroyed. Mirrors must not be allowed to spill out their stored secrets. Even during uneventful times, very young children are not allowed to look in a mirror. This time the prohibition concerns children's abilities to perceive things that adults may not. The reflective side of a mirror is a place of mystery, and in it things appear that grown-up eyes are blind to. In case of youngsters, nonetheless, those things are still visible.

Arguably, such an object is not to be taken lightly. Careless gazing in the Mongolian looking-glass is unwise. To check their appearance, when needed, people use small hand mirrors instead. And that with caution. Parents advise their children not to look at their reflections too often. There is a fear of losing oneself in the mirror. Not, as Humphrey writes referring to Rebecca Empson, in the way that Narcissus lost himself, but lose one self by becoming attached to "'another self,'" not that of the real world.[5] It is a fear mostly associated with the other side: the world beyond the mirror of which only passing shadows and flashing lights we sometimes notice. That is, we think, an idea close to Borges' mirror people – close, but not the same (see Chapter 6). In fact, there is a profound difference between the two: we accept the idea of Borges' mirror people (a world populated with persons similar to us, existing at the other side of the mirror in which we look) as 'fiction', that is something that could not 'really' affect us. But in the case of the Buryats the threat is real. It is real because it matters and has important consequences for the Buryats' modes of being. With the fictional mirror, we are able to immerse our self into the enchanted world of reflection, to get a glimpse into extraordinary places beyond the glass. We allow our self to be astonished by stories of living mirrors, mirrors possessed by vengeful spirits or mirrors that are shiny portals to all kinds of terrors. And yet, even though we cross, in our imagination, the borders of the looking-glass, the borders hold. What we experience – the unworldly, fascinating beasts; the upside down universes; the angry ghosts – are safely trapped inside the mirror, which is in turn safely stored inside the confines of literature or film or any other media.[6] The thrill can reach us, but the dangers cannot. The fantasy mirror is a mirror made of words, enacted in our imagination. It is a relatively safe adventure – a sort of an 'imaginary enchantment': enchantment in the tamed setting of make-believe, a rose without thorns.

For the Buryats of Western Mongolia, it is a rather different story. The captivating, and at times threatening, interiority of the mirror leaks into the real world. To them, the fantasy mirror and the real mirror are one and the same object. The mirror's enchantment that we, in our modern world, have pushed back and locked inside a specific literary genre is perilous and unrestrained. We are now on a land of permeable borders.

The world at the other side of the mirror

The world of the living and the world of the dead in Mongolia have a border that, according to Humphrey's ethnography, can be crossed from either side. The two worlds can glance into each other through a shaman's mirror.[7] Visibility for those on either side is a play of shadows and dazzling images: a story of light and darkness. The shamanic mirror allows visibility among the living and the dead. As a material agent, the shaman's mirror, the *toli*, can act as a portal, a weapon and a shield. A living person glances from outside into it. The opposite way is the way of the dead. Spirits look from inside the mirror at the world outside and at us. They see us as creatures, 'red worms of the Sunny World' (*nartyn ulaan horhod*).[8] The living seems soft to them, small and lacking in physical ability. People in Mongolia are aware of the invisible world beyond the mirror. A regular person though may rarely catch the image of the dead into the mirror's glittering surface. Only shamans enter their world and they do so through their mirrors.

Shamans, that can be either males or females, are human beings possessed by spirits. Therefore, shamans, at certain times, can be spirits.[9] Unlike household mirrors, shamanic mirrors are made entirely of polished metal (brass or bronze) and then covered with patina. A metal loop is placed on the inside from which the mirror can be hung. The indigenous mirror of Inner Asia is usually undecorated. Those manufactured in China have various depictions which include animals, the five elements and themes from Chinese mythology. China, in particular, had a great tradition in producing and exporting metallic mirrors, especially bronze. Those mirrors were mainly used for ritual purposes in China – for burials, ancestral worship or as gifts in weddings. But there is a type of Chinese mirror known as a magic mirror or more precisely as a 'light penetrating mirror' (*tou guang jing*). Exposed to light, the characters and images on the back of such a mirror would reflect on the wall, as if they can pass through it.[10] Humphrey states that probably indigenous mirrors of south Siberian-Mongolian region predate those manufactured in China. 'For Mongols, however, the "ancientness" of shaman's mirrors points not to their particular historical or geographical origins but to the timeless, 'always-ness' of shamanic practice among humans'.[11]

All shamanic mirrors in Mongolia have a rather blotchy and murky surface, slightly curved, able to produce a dim, distorted image. No matter how polished its shiny side is, the reflection the shaman's mirror produces is always clouded.[12] Still, the word *toli* is used to describe both the household glass mirror and the shamanic mirror. The word means encyclopaedia or a place for the storage of knowledge. The use of the same word indicates that, in theory, even without glass the shaman's mirror can dazzle the eye, cast light and reflect things in it.[13]

Because the reflection offered by the *toli* is distorted and clouded, Humphrey writes, the mirror of the shaman is in itself a challenge as to what constitutes a reflection. What one sees inside the *toli* is defined by who is looking.

Like the mirrors all over the world, the shamanic mirror has two distinctive sides: one polished and a dull, insipid one. What is most striking, however, about the Mongolian mirror is that both of its sides are in use. The polished one for reflecting things and the other side as a portal to a darker world: the world of the dead. Now, how does that world look like? To the living, it is a world deprived of light. Nothing really exists there, neither life and beauty nor happiness and destiny. It is a dark void where everything becomes lost. Beams of light, which are the souls of the dead, occasionally light up the darkness. The land of the dead, which is identical to our own apart from its obscurity, is visible only to shamans in trance and to people in dreaming, but only shamans may purposefully venture in and out of that world through their mirrors. Shamans journey the dark world bravely but with caution, sometimes bringing messages to the dead from the living or delivering wishes and counsel from the dead to the sunny world. There is a variety of spirit-like beings. Chthonic spirits, Humphrey states, might take residence in water, rocks, trees, ancestors and shamans. There are also malevolent lesser beings that sometimes originate of human souls and none of them establish a unified category. Shamans in Darhad and Horcin, nevertheless, deal mostly with *ongons*, powerful spirits thought to be the souls of the once-living people that died under tragic and extraordinary circumstances or had lived in them. Therefore, they might be angry, unsatisfied or wanting to take revenge. Mongolian spirits like these cannot be countless or endlessly shifting shapes. They are counted for, reside in specific places and have known narratives.

So, on the other side of the mirror, 'there seem to be degrees of human-focused intensity. There are varied, nameless, running, floating, wriggling invisible powers, which are the activations of countless spirits as well as impure objects, unknown corpses and maleficent curses.'[14] But there are also shamans' *ongons*, named and familiar, and people dare not to neglect them. If they do, a shaman *ongon* might become malignant and bring misfortune and pain to the community. On the other hand, if people take care of them through constant offerings and rituals, shamans' *ongons* can provide good fortune, health and fertility. In Mongolia ghosts are not exactly nonhumans. They may have supernatural powers like immortality, invisibility, multiplicity – they can even become human again, for a while, possessing a human body. Spirits change shapes and can move constantly through special tracks called *güidel* without leaving a trace, but they are still the souls of former human beings and so they share the same psychology. That means they have feelings. The dead in Mongolia can be happy or sad, angry or frightened. They eat and drink and, like people, they need company. Not to be lonely, spirits may snatch living souls to be with them.

In a world where countless spirits lurk on the other side of the mirror, the borders between life and death are, according to Humphrey, not clearly set. There is death which is not absolute death and life which is not exactly life. Dreaming, for instance, is a time when body and soul temporarily separate; illness is also a period of similar division. It is considered natural that the soul of a person is not constantly with them. It may travel away from the body, wonder around and pay visits to other spirits. If the soul will not return, the person dies. Apparently, hazy borders cannot guarantee one's protection from the potential intrusion of the supernatural. Interactions are more than possible: they are inevitable. A curious space between life and death has been created in the absence of firm boundaries, and in that space the living are vulnerable. The soul of a person might have an unfortunate encounter with a vengeful spirit as it travels far from its body or is captured by a lonely ghost. Actually, Mongols think that each human being has many souls. Three is the number believed by many to be the most accurate. Every person has three souls: one perishes with the physical body; another lingers after death around the body and the world of the living, but only for a while. The third soul may pass after death to the other world or choose to be reborn as an infant.

As the borders of life and death are not closed from either side, a person can be dead but not quite so or alive but not really. An aliveness that is not alive might mean a man or woman possessed by a spirit. Almost dead, somewhat dead, might imply a person whose soul is indeed away from its physical body and so it appears to be dead, but the soul may not be far or irretrievably away. A shaman will be called for the soul to be rescued, retrieved and reclaimed. To mediate the space between life and death, the shaman will use and depend on their mirror. The mirror will be the portal, the armour and the weapon. Sometimes it may even be the vessel on which the shaman will fly to battle.

Portal, weapon, shield

The shamanic mirror has the ability to move and affect lives, to destroy or reveal psychic energy. Sometimes, as Humphrey suggests citing Otgony Purev, it can even seem to mysteriously act on its own.[15] The mirror has a spirit given to it by blood. In a rite called *amiluulah*, a spirit passes into the mirror's metal. A sheep or goat is slaughtered, a spirit is called and the mirror is then dipped into the blood for the spirit to pass in it and give it life.

A shaman makes sure that every three years the mirror is 'blooded' to keep on living. The spirit nests in the inner side of the mirror, along with other invited spirits or even the spirit of the possessed shaman. Thus, the mirror is a portal and a container. Then, the mirror travels. It roams under the earth or rolls by itself on its surface, cutting through paths and roads in a mysterious cross-way manner called *hündelen yavan*.[16] The mirror can also offer a ride to its shaman and to other spirits. Its curved side is now offered for souls to ride as if on a boat.

As souls and possessed shamans ride on mirrors and vengeful ghosts venture among the living, people need protection: someone to negotiate constantly the fragile relationship of the living and the dead and travel the vast expanse of the dark world. That person is the shaman. Viveiros de Castro defined shamanism as 'the capacity evinced by some individuals to cross ontological boundaries deliberately and adopt the perspective of nonhuman subjectivities in order to administer the relations between humans and nonhumans'.[17] Humphrey claims that if we substitute the word 'nonhumans' with the word 'spirits', the description fits perfectly the Mongolian shaman. She describes how the shaman mediates the two worlds using his or her mirror for divination and as a vital part of their performance. During their rites, shamans wore their mirrors like armour. He or she places them on and around their bodies having the polished side facing outwards. Often, they use several mirrors, as is the case with the Daurs who use a heart mirror worn in front of their bodies and another one worn on their backs. The number of mirrors shamans use is indicative of their powers and they can have up to thirteen. As they perform they are located within their mirrors. So, the mirrors contain the shamans as well as guard them against evil forces. The mirror repels curses and attacks from enemy spirits, and, in that case, it is thought to act as a shield.

To travel the dark world of the dead, shamans perform mostly at night. They do so with their eyes closed in order to see as spirits, adopting their point of view. 'In the country of the blind, one should close one's eyes, in the land of the lame, one should walk with a bent leg.'[18] Closing their eyes shamans concentrate their power, resist desire and adopt the position of the spirits they are about to encounter. But not all of them do. Sometimes, shamans in a trance keep their eyes open, and when they do, their eyes are considered extremely dangerous. The eyes of the shamans are possessed by spirits. They are capable of emitting frightening rays of light and their gaze can be damaging to ordinary people. In the Horchin area shamans hide their eyes behind a black cloth to protect the people around them.[19] In fact, Mongols relate the eyes of the shaman with the mirror: both have the power to absorb things from the outside, store them inside them and then cast them out again. Open or closed, the shaman's eyes do not see. It is the mirror that 'sees'. In fact, as we read in Humphrey's work, the shaman might even be travelling with his or her eyes closed and still be able to see adopting the position of the spirit inside the mirror. As the mirror becomes a weapon casting flashes of light, so become the eyes of the shaman. The eyes become the mirror, and the mirror becomes the eyes. The shaman's gaze is, therefore, the gaze of the mirror.

Perhaps, hiding the shaman's eyes behind a cloth falls under the same principle, and offers the same protection, as when a household glass mirror is covered up during a death in the family. Still, operating from both of its sides, the Mongolian mirror is not to be trusted. If a corpse is reflected in it, the soul of the dead person can be trapped inside. The dead person from inside the mirror will then be able to gaze outside of it and watch his or her family, becoming thus unwilling to abandon the world of the living.[20] In the same manner but from the other side, living people might look in the mirror and catch images of the world of the dead. The mirror, therefore, with its dual function, is thought to provide glimpses of what is through or behind it; it does not end at its back side. On the contrary, a whole world lies on the other side of the mirror. That world sometimes opens up even to the gaze of ordinary people. To transport the Mongolian mirror into Carroll's novels, a 'real' Alice could accidentally 'step through' a shamanic mirror. Only the world she would have encountered might have been terrifying. And it wouldn't have been a dream. Or better still, since the soul is considered in Mongolia to travel during sleep in the transcendental land beyond the mirror, her dream would be much real.

When someone dies in Mongolia, Humphrey writes, a shaman might be called to try to travel the darkness and bring back the soul of the departed, but if that proves impossible, final death arrives and the body starts to disintegrate. Yet, some souls do not depart. They become ghosts and haunt the living. Other souls turn to *ongon* spirits. Such transformations take time to be accomplished. The flesh on the corpse should vanish completely and the shaman would then be called to perform rites in which the spirit would be recognized and named. In future rites, the spirit might be summoned to aid the living. However, not all spirits are kind and willing to help. Some may attack, and, in such a case, the shamanic mirror becomes a weapon protecting its owner. To fight off enemies, the mirror emanates flashes of dazzling light. Spirits are also made of light and fight by it. They are visible to shamans as illuminations surrounded by absolute darkness and attack mostly during the night.

Mongolia is a place of contrasting light and darkness, the light belongs to the living and the darkness is the realm of the dead. The night, thus, is a time when the universe is out of balance – now the living are in the dark – and the living are more vulnerable for it.[21] The light spirits emanate may be blue, white or red. It is never a normal kind of light. Shamans are always able to see the light of spirits. Ordinary people do not. Yet, the light of the mirror is sometimes visible to everyone: when mirrors are travelling distances on their own, they appear blazing. The mirror is not only a weapon. It is also an instrument of healing. For instance, the shaman may wipe the smooth side of the mirror on the body of an ill person to restore health. Nevertheless, the shamanic mirror can be sent from far away to cause great harm.

Daunting mirror

There was once a young man in Mongolia who quarrelled with a shaman. The two men lived in distant villages. The shaman sent his mirror to attack and punish the young man. The mirror flew through the night sky, found the house of the young man in his far away village and entered it through the window. The young man though was prepared. He was awake waiting, and even though he could not see the mirror he saw a blue light coming into the house. Because the man was strong and ready the mirror did not assault him. Instead, the mirror sensed weakness in his wife who was at that time asleep in the same room. The man saw the blue light sitting on his wife and his wife died. The next morning the man put his dead woman in a cupboard (which he used as a coffin) and took her to the countryside. But the shaman did not let it end there. Every night he went to the woman's resting place, beating his drum and performing on top of her coffin in order to steal her spirit.

Unable to tolerate the shaman's behaviour any longer, and seeking revenge, the young man secretly removed the body of his dead wife from her coffin. He took its place inside it, waiting for the shaman to come. Indeed, the shaman returned as he did every night and started performing and chanting. Abruptly, the young man jumped out of the coffin and attacked. The shaman was so frightened that he fell ill and died with his heart broken. But the young's man fate was not much better. Because he spent the night in a coffin, he became mad. Nobody won. The story of the feud between the young, bold man and the shaman was told to Humphrey by Hürelbaatar (as Humphrey states in her article) and it concerns the people of the Horchin region. It points the use of the mirror as shaman's weapon. Also, it highlights the visibility of the mirror as a blue light, its ability to fly, its willingness to act at the shaman's commands, and of course, the danger of death and madness inevitably involved with the shamanic mirror. The story hints at the real hazard associated with mirrors and meddling with concepts such as life and death (the young man loses his mind because he takes the place of a dead person in the coffin while being alive). Understandably, people are very reluctant to look in a shamanic mirror or having it placed inside their home – if a shaman could die as a result of interacting with his mirror, imagine what could happen to an ordinary person. A better place for a shamanic mirror is sometimes considered to be outside the house, above the doorway, for the mirror to repel curses and misfortune. Still, even in such cases, the mirror would be wrapped in cloth.

Mongolia is not the only place where people demonstrate fear in the presence or use of a mirror. An intercultural association of the mirror with the supernatural is hard not to be noticed: the mirror acting as a portal to a different, darker world, or nesting malevolent spirits and monsters inside its depths. Stories compete with each other to prove it. Even far from the shamans of Mongolia, we come across superstitious narratives in which the mirror is potentially harmful. The seven years of bad luck upon the breaking of the mirror, the dangers of looking into a mirror after dark, the images of the dead that may very well appear in the mirror on New Year Eve, all have to do with an unworldly association of the mirror and the human soul. The breaking of the mirror brings seven unfortunate years because the mirror reflects one's soul and so, along with the glass, the soul is broken to pieces. It takes seven years for a soul to heal, so, the person whose mirror is broken will be safe again in the same amount of time. It is said that grinding the mirror into dust, burying the mirror or tapping the broken mirror on a gravestone is said to prevent the bad luck.[22]

But who said it?

Perhaps instinctively, we attribute dangerous qualities to our own self-inspection. We make up stories that seem to cut across cultures and their origins are hard to trace.[23] In ancient Greece the mirror was forbidden to men, at least, for self-inspecting reasons.[24] The mirror was considered to be a dangerous object as it might entrap a man into himself – as it happened to Narcissus – or turn him into an object, a thing, through the inevitable identification of one's self with one's self-reflection. Clearly, a man's role was to be a sociable and extrovert being. Self-inspection in a mirror and self-beautification in front of a mirror, therefore, were considered to be inferior, dangerous and vain behaviours adequate only for women. The mirror was granted only to women because, as Francoise Frontisi-Ducroux and Jean-Pierre Vernant write, their fate was entrapment – in a man's house and in their roles as wives or daughters. So, to be objectified through the act of looking in the mirror was, for women, almost natural. Furthermore, becoming entrapped in the mirror adequately reflected a woman's destiny. The mirror and the short-sighted view of the world it offers to its observer belonged to women, since men had to be able to look beyond their noses – out into society and their fellow citizens.

The main metaphor for the mirror's entrapment was that of the maze or the labyrinth. 'Like the mirror, the labyrinth originates in a paradoxical negation: it is a path that, literally going nowhere, is essentially pathless.'[25] The victim of a labyrinth, Willard McCarty writes, is forced or beguiled to repeat the same movement, either physically or imaginatively. Thus, the victim is trapped. McCarty claims that catoptric fascination works in a similar fashion: by offering to the observer immediate repetition of their movements it encourages the same aimless 'wondering'. For McCarty, movement can be seen as a metaphor for thought, so, 'the labyrinth can be regarded as the outer form of the victim's inner state, his confusion of mind. Thus we can speak of the catoptric labyrinth and the labyrinthine mirror.[26]

We have referred many times in this book to an idea repeatedly connected with the mirror: that of a world existing through and beyond it. McCarty leads us there again by discussing Roman poet and philosopher Lucretius and his likening of the mirror observer with a man in a house gazing through an opening to a reality beyond.[27] Lucretius's metaphor, according to McCarty, perfectly encapsulates the main view of the mirror in antiquity as a portal into a world beyond human vision and reach. More interestingly, McCarty points out that Lucretius, with his metaphor, underlines the occurrence of an individual being aware of gazing out 'from the bony house of the skull into a world reachable only through the senses. Thus, paradoxically, the metaphor suggests not only access to the interior world of essences but also entrapment within the limits of the self.'[28]

Because of this negative attitude towards the mirror as an instrument of entrapment, men were not supposed to use it. McCarty provides us with the case of Apuleius who had to defend himself, in the middle of the second-century AD, for using a mirror by referring to its value in terms of self-knowledge. Mirror gazing, on the other hand, was appropriated to women mostly for beautification and erotic purposes. As always, outlandish stories followed the use of the mirror. Aristotle offers a detailed and curious account on the relationship between the mirror and the female body.[29] When women are looking into the mirror while having their periods, Aristotle claims, a sort of bloody cloud appears on the looking-glass. That bloody stain is not easy to be removed from the mirror, especially if the mirror is brand new. That happens because the eyes of a woman, just like any other organ of the female body, have veins. So, during a menstrual flow, the female eyes, like the rest of her organs, change and become infected with blood – a change not visible to other people. The eyes, consequently, set the air in motion and act upon it by causing it to do the same thing (an inflammation of blood) that they endure. That happens because the eyes are shiny so they are not only influenced by the air, but, in return, can affect the air. The layer of air which exists on top of the mirror's surface, then, in its turn, influences the mirror, thus the bloody mist on its surface.

To put it simply, according to Aristotle, a woman transmits the blood of her menstrual flow through her eyes, into the air, and then onto the mirror in which she gazes. The blood stain of the female menstrual flow that is transmitted on the mirror's surface, through her gaze, is not easy to be cleaned because it penetrates the mirror deeply and in every direction. The smoother the mirror, the worse will be the stain. Consistent with this theory, the gaze acts as it is acted upon. Pliny, the Roman naturalist, agrees that Aristotle's views were commonplace in his time. In his work he also mentions that, if a woman gazes in a mirror while having her menstrual flow, the brightness of the mirror would be affected and its glass would become foggy.[30] Nevertheless, if the woman looks again in the mirror on its back side, the mirror regains its shine. So, the female gaze acts in the opposite direction and removes the mist from the mirror, just like a hammer would do, striking the metal from the opposite direction. For Aristotle and Pliny, a woman's gaze during menstruation carried her blood through the air in tiny red particles. The female bloody gaze was, therefore, a well-kept secret that only mirror could reveal. In essence, what the mirror made visible, once a woman's gaze fells upon it, was her womb.

A dark glimpse

The mirror does not provoke fear, excitement or unease, solely because of metaphysical association and outlandish stories. That the mirror reveals the unseen is an obvious fact. We do not have to consider ghosts and spirit-worlds, but merely our own face, visible to us only through our mirror reflection. The reason an ordinary person in Mongolia finds the experience of looking in reflecting surfaces uncomfortable enough is, primarily, not that different to our own. According to Humphrey, it has to do with one's complicated relationship with one's self and the relationship of self and other.[31] Mirrors 'problematise looking and touching, image and substance ...'.[32] The following Mongolian riddle gives indications of the trouble nature of these relations:

It makes one into two
Nameless and white.[33]

Indeed, 'Nameless and white', can easily come to mind when pondering on a mirror's reflection. It suggests, if we attempt an interpretation of our own, the division between self and mirrored self. It also points to the loss of personal identity one suffers in front of the mirror, as the living body becomes a thing: a reflection without name.

Still, the distinct quality of the Mongolian shamanic mirror does not lie in what is actually seen in its hardly polished, reflective surface. As Humphrey points out, the mirror 'disturbs and places under question what "seeing" and "reflecting" are ... the shaman's mirror is an instrument whose design encourages a progression of thoughts: looking at, looking into, and looking through (the mirror).'[34] So, while the Mongolian mirror puzzles the relationship of self and mirroring as much as any other mirror, it is also there to give us hints, to make us look differently. We believe that it suggests an alternative way of gazing. What one sees on its surface is not a clear fact – the 'silver and precise' reflection of Sylvia Plath's mirror. On the contrary, Mongolian mirrors are made to give reflections that are unique and unclear, therefore, open to interpretation.

What needs to be interpreted is not necessarily the reflection of a human body. According to anthropologist Katherine Swancutt,[35] during mirror divinations in Bayandun, shamans, after murmuring invocations to spirits, pour vodka on their mirrors and exhale over them. Then, together with the people who are gathered there, they try to make out and interpret the filmy shape that appears on the mirrors once the vodka dries out.[36] Understandably, the shape is rarely as apparent as to be beyond debate. The people, though, need to understand what kind of being is evident in the shape, so as to know which spirit is responsible for their misfortunes. The shamans in Horchin, on the other hand, do not use vodka or any other liquid but simply stare into the mirror. The purpose, as always, is to see beyond the hazy reflections of the polished metal: to see through. With luck, beings on the other side of the mirror can become visible. In rare occasions, the spirit-world may open up even to the gaze of ordinary people. This is called 'to glimpse through a glass darkly'.[37]

Now, what might be revealed through such mirror gazes? The whole point is, of course, to see something that we weren't supposed to see; something that, by all means, shouldn't have been there – an impossibility that will create the link to 'prospective possibilities, producing the basis for innovations which initially appear to arise out of nothing'.[38] This might be a reflection or a stain far from perfect, that would make one think for a long time and will initiate, as Swancutt tells us, 'a process of innovation wherein repeated questioning leads to combinatory thought which imposes novel combinations on people, who perceive the need for innovation, access an innovation, and finally recursively posit that innovation's conceptual origins'.[39] In a way, the Mongolian mirror is a mirror only in principle. It becomes a conceptual mirror. Enigmatic and utterly obscure, it mostly offers, we think, a guess at shapes. Unlike the mirror we are used to, we are now face to face with a 'secretive' object made of a dimly reflective substance that affords traces of meaning to be discovered, rather than reflections to be seen. That is to have reached a point where not only the reflection of our face is not of any particular importance, but the point where a definite and clear mirroring becomes a burden.

Hazy shapes and metaphors

For the Mongolians who performed the mirror divination of the previous example, the vodka left a trace on the mirror that, at first glance, looked like a bird to Swancutt.[40] Yet, as she writes, her interpretation was disputed by Galanjav, the head of one of the allied families who feared that shamans from rival families had put a curse on them. Other family members, however, took Swancutt's interpretation into account during a second reading which revealed the shape of the lama-shaman (a shaman from a rival family). The conclusion reached combined the initial suspicion of the curse with the shape of the bird in what Swancutt calls 'combinatory thought'[41] – a less restrictive way of thinking that allows for innovation and novel combination: The lama-shaman had used a nature spirit (in the form of a chicken) to cause harm. So, while a hazy shape can invite various meanings, it can only have one right meaning for a specific person or occasion: a meaning that will lead to problem solving. Reading Swancutt's ethnography we might assume that looking, in this instance, has less to do with seeing and more with realizing, with building up sense. And for the purpose of our chapter, keep in mind that the Mongolian mirror hints at interpreting a reflection by thinking beyond the mirror's frame.

What we 'see' does not necessarily have to be on the mirror's surface. To gaze in the mirror is to explore a multiplicity and variety of possibilities: meaning that comes in many forms.

What we learn here is nothing less than an alternative way of looking into the mirror. To experiment with it, we decided to look in a mirror (the 'mirror' here can be any shiny, reflective surface, also, an old mirror would be better than a new one) trying to interpret anything that exists on it, other than our faces. Unlike the Buryats we live in a world where the borders between life and death, spirits and persons, are clearly defined and impenetrable. For us, to gaze in our imaginary Mongolian mirror is to be searching for a metaphor; an 'as if' that would bestow us with vision beyond reflection. So, we gazed in the mirror not to see our reflection, but to see beyond and through it. The experiment was simple: we looked for any shape except of our own faces.

Exploring the metaphor-building potential of mirror gazing, 'glimpsing darkly' in the mirror produced, for us, an unclear, diaphanous silhouette: an old, foggy stain that we noticed at the left corner of the glass. We tried several interpretations. Some seemed unfit or irrelevant. We skipped them. Finally, a shape became certain: that is, certain to us and for the purpose of this book. One shape cannot fit all. Everyone is invited to take part in this mirror-gazing experiment, to find their own metaphor and reach meaning through their own mirror-gazing experience. Nevertheless, our metaphor took the shape of a deer – an elegant, red deer, like the ones native to Scotland, or perhaps to the Caucasus Mountains and Asia.

The deer was trapped. It had been captured inside our mirror with no way to escape. It looked unaware of its entrapment, strong and at the same time vulnerable. To be honest, that was hardly surprising. A deer had been stubbornly following us for a while now. In the introduction of this book, it hesitantly approached the mirror we deliberately placed in the middle of a forest. It stood there for a while facing its reflection. In Chapter 4, it was waiting for us in a world without names, without a clear 'I'. It helped us to realize that, in such a world, we could have existed together without fear. Later on, the deer appeared unexpectedly in the mirror as we were staring purposefully in it. It looked as surprised to be there as we were to find it. So, the deer had been tracing us, in one way or another, buried up to its neck in the lines of this book. It will later become clear why a deer, an animal of prey, appeared trapped in our mirror as we were looking for a metaphor. In this chapter, however, the captured deer is dead. But not quite. The Mongolian mirror operates in a place where the line between life and death is indiscernible. So, we interpreted the shape in the mirror as a deer that belongs to the world of the dead, but also has a presence in the world of the living: a deer in a natural history museum, dead, but not entirely non-existent.

More precisely, the deer that came to our minds looking in the mirror was one we had visited in Oxford's Natural History museum: a red stag that used to stand at the entrance's right side, along with a leopard and a brown bear. It used to be standing there, proud and tall and dead, for all the visitors to see – a sign next to it read: please touch. We did touch. The deer's fur was soft but eerie cold. The presence of that deer, like any animal in a natural history museum, was confusing. Even though lifeless, it had a physical presence which was undeniable. Its image testified to an animal staring in the distance as if ready to move. It looked like a living deer. The children around it approached and touched it merrily in a way they would never treat a corpse. But in the end, no matter how alive it looked, or how beautiful, it was just that: a corpse. To paraphrase our next Mongolian riddle: if you looked, it was like a deer; if you thought about it, it was like a corpse. This brings us to our next point.

Thinking dead

If you look, it is like a person.
If you think, it is like a corpse.[42]

We find the distinction of the above riddle between the 'looker' and the 'thinker' when it comes to a mirror observer particularly telling. First of all, it connects to the point we try to make in this book: the distinction between the one who just looks into the mirror and the one who thinks deeply with and through it. Moreover, it expresses the possibility of discovering new modes of existence through mirror gazing. For the Mongolian shamans, in particular, the riddle can take a literal meaning. The dead (spirits or ghosts) may appear in the mirror for the thinker (the shaman, we might assume, as opposed to the ordinary person) as unfamiliar possibilities become thinkable in the new place in which the shamanic mirror operates. In that horizon, according to Humphrey, the system of physical existence with its laws and regulations ceases to function. Things that appear in the mirror have different, hidden meanings. What is at issue, Humphrey observes, is nothing less than the 'eternal question of the truth of being'.[43] It is one thing, Humphrey continues, to accept the existence of many perspectives (of animals, of people, of the dead) and quite another to accept that those statements are equal or that any of them says something true. That possibility is horrifying. For if the perspective of the dead in the land beyond the mirror holds any value, then, the living (us) might as well be red worms, inhabiting a world of darkness. In addition, to extend Humphrey's line of thought to a previous chapter of our book and to the realms of literature, perhaps the possibility of an alien perspective being true holds the same agony that overcame Alice when Tweedledum and Tweedledee happily suggested to her, as they watched the comical figure of the snoring Red King, that she might not be real, and that she only exists inside the Red King's dream.

Away from Mongolia and into our modern world, however, we do not suffer such agonies. There are no ghosts inside our mirrors. Dead people do not roam on the other side of its glass. And yet, our mirror might still have something to say to a 'thinker' about death. That is, it might reflect what we believe about our death and the meaning it has for us. We are referring to the prospect of how we think about the mirror shapes, in some respect, the way we think of our existence. So, perhaps there might be opportunities to gain knowledge from a corpse inside our household mirror without breaking our ontological borders or escaping into the world of fiction. Such an opportunity is well illustrated by philosopher Raymond Tallis in his book *The Black Mirror*.[44] Tallis has a simple proposition for his reader. To explain it, he is talking to himself, and he calls himself 'RT'. In fact, while looking into the mirror, Tallis is talking to his future corpse. He invites us to do the same. Naked in front of the looking-glass, Tallis sees an image that is 'an earlier time-slice of the item that will be your corpse, a time slice that, unlike the later one, is looking back at you.'[45]

In front of the mirror Tallis contemplates on his future corpse. The body that is facing him, as he stands in front the mirror, is indeed the one that would be shown to whoever comes to pay their last respect in the event of his death. It is the body that, as Tallis imagines, will be lifted by nurses and laid down in that special place in the hospital. The body from which any personal items will be removed: eye glasses, wedding rings, watches – a body beyond and out of time. What had once been a person is, under Tallis' gaze, now transformed into an 'it', alone and deprived of everything, absent and cold. Nurses will eventually wash that body one last time, making sure they attend all rules of hygiene. Its hair will be brushed, its teeth will be washed, the arms – that very arms we see in front of us in the mirror will be lifted and folded across the chest. The hands will be clasped together; the eyes will be closed. The idea of the *Black Mirror* is to be awakened by death and appreciate having an embodied self and a conscious existence. RT is looking at his mirrored self and sees the very lifeless head that will be lifted up on a pillow, the chin that will be propped up 'to prevent the mouth falling open in a silent scream'[46] and the lips that a nurse will coat with Vaseline to keep them moist as the tongue is now useless. The very feet that are always aware of the body's weight as we stand in front of the mirror will be unable to feel anything, their connection to the environment forever severed and lost. Their last step taken.

Tallis considers death as the ultimate certainty of life. The reflection of his corpse in the mirror reminds him of the long process between birth and death – the inevitability of death casting an ironic shadow on the deep worries and endless preoccupations of life. He thinks of his parents. How many times and on how many different occasions they were concerned about him. His parents worrying through his childhood: bed-time stories, illnesses, nutrition, safety. Then, the schooling years, exams, bullying, grades, successes and failures, married years, professional career: all those long periods of detailed anxieties leading nowhere but to an upward road towards the edge of a cliff. Parents tell their children to keep away from edges, RT contemplates, and yet one day the edge will come for us and for our children just the same. The absolute nothingness that follows is beyond comprehension. We may try to think of it as we stare at our reflection. Gazing into the eyes that one day will be gaze-less.

All that insight Tallis gains from the 'dead' in the mirror. Instead of communicating with spirits, as a shaman might do, Tallis simply imagines himself dead. The mirror, in any context, is an object to think with, through and about. RT's mirror gaze offers a deep thinking of death and of what it steals from the living, but it also suggests, even unintentionally, a way in which a 'modern' mirror could be inhabited by the dead: what in the future will be our corpse, the same eyes, the same face, is looking at us through the looking-glass. And this is where the story ends. It ends there because our modern mirror terminates on the wall on which it hangs. There is absolutely nothing beyond the mirror and, therefore, death brings about an absolute nothingness. We think through things and imagine through them. Tallis's black mirror, our mirror, with its rigid borders, affords very little in terms of imagining a horizon that exists after death for us to step into. Truth is, if we thought of our mirror as a portal, a potential doorway to the world of the dead, Tallis's narrative would be different. His death, in his mind, would be different.

Lonely glass

Now let's think a bit more of Tallis's narrative. Tallis invites us to find our future corpse in the mirror: to imagine our mirrored body lifeless, emotionless, joyless, breathless, selfless. But do we really have to use our imagination in order to see a dead thing in the mirror? Tallis's imaginary view of his future corpse points to what the mirror does to all of us anyway: turns us into objects. Tallis describes the transition from life to death as a long journey from I-hood to object-hood. Still, looking into the mirror is a very short journey from 'I' to 'it'. In other words, inside our mirror we die every day. We do not have to imagine our future corpses to see a reflection with no pulse, no blood and no organs. By definition, a mirror reflection is lifeless. This might not be something we take notice of, or contemplate on, but it happens every time we turn our gaze at the looking-glass – an unceremonious transition from a felt, embodied self, an 'I', into a thing, an 'it'. Unlike the mirrors of Mongolia, our mirror is made specifically to reflect our face, as clearly as it can be done. We do not use the mirror to envisage ideas of personhood or to interpret shapes, but to find a cloudless, lifeless mirrored body. In a way, our mirror guides us to identify with our future corpse. It coaches us to become a spiritless object.

Another distinctive difference: our mirror is not borderless. In contrast to the shamanic mirror, it ends abruptly at its back side. Only the front side of our mirror is in use and past that side, there is no door to another world. Our modern mirror provides a cruel border: not one that separates two things, but a border with nothing beyond. Standing in front of it, the world is all about us and in it we are alone. The phenomenology of our mirror imposes and, at the same time, reflects faithfully the borders marked on our existence: in finality, our mirror and our death reflect each other. For the Buryats of Mongolia, the end of the mirror, its back side, is also the beginning of the world of the dead. Accordingly, death is considered to be the start of another kind of existence: the beginning of an infinite life in an alternate universe.

The Mongolian mirror reflects an open ending. In comparison, our own mirror stands deprived of spirits, of 'beneath', or 'beyond'. It is a lonely glass, sanitized of souls and ghosts clinically reflecting our bodies. Of course, facing our mirror we are safe – no beaming *ongons* would stare back at us, no lethal, enemy mirror can fly towards us from afar with a dark purpose. In short, no disorienting question about the truth of our existence. Tragic events are not deposited inside the mirror's depths to haunt us or expose us in the future. With our secular mirror we are secure. But there's nowhere to go. Our safety is paid for with a definite and unmovable line we cannot extend ourselves beyond. Modern mirrors offer no escape from life, from death, from self. There is no release. Death in our mirror is irrevocable. A dead person reflected in it could never stare back at us, be tempted to stay around us for a little longer or be free to move on. It would only produce the lifeless reflection of someone that has already died: a dead in our mirror would be twice as dead.

This is our mirror's perspective. Since there are no spirits in it, the mirror can only afford a view through the lifeless eyes of our reflection: no after-life illusions, no possibility of another land with rivers and forests and ancestors waiting to welcome us on the other side. In a manner of speaking, and while we are still alive, we are already the ghosts inside our modern mirror.

Part Three

Hunters and Prey

The mirror trap

Self-hunting

This chapter is an invitation to a hunting adventure. It asks of you to think of mirroring on a par with snaring. That is, to think of the mirror as a device for the remote capture of prey. First, some things about traps: traps are usually designed to catch particular animals. They target their habits and predict the ways they move in the landscape and forge their paths in it. A good trap, like a good hunter, is adapted to the distinctive features of its prey. Traps are mute; they do not speak. Yet, they do signify and communicate, in the language of material signs, information about the animals' strengths and weaknesses. Traps enact and objectify relevant parts of the hunter's knowledge on the animals' whereabouts and landscaping activities; how they go about to discover food, mates or water. It is no secret among hunters that the more the trap knows or remembers about the prey the more effective it is.

There are many kinds of traps as there are different kinds of prey. Prey can be broadly divided into two categories: aware and unaware prey. Aware prey denotes animals with knowledge or previous experience of traps as devices able to ensnare or kill. Unaware prey denotes animals with no such previous knowledge or understanding. Most animals are unaware victims. Humans can be both. Self-consciousness seems to be the major criterion of differentiation. Unfortunately, for prey, traps exist for both kinds. This distinction has very little to do with the chances that the prey is captured or it escapes. Traps for animals with a predilection for self-consciousness, however, are different.

What about the mirror then? How exactly does the mirror trap work? What turns this everyday object into a hunting weapon? What creatures is it designed to catch? Who is the hunter and what is the prey? The argument we want to put forward in this chapter is that mirrors are traps especially designed for sentient creatures of the self-conscious kind. The major assumption is that the mirror trap enacts 'in the wild' the same basic principles of the so-called mirror self-recognition test that has been used for studying self-identification in the laboratories of developmental and animal psychology.[1] In other words, the operation of the mirror trap is grounded on the ability of the mirror to act as a self-recognition device. We will show that the mirror resembles a powerful attractor within a dynamic semiotic field of subjectification and self-identification. Specifically, the mirror trap operates primarily on the basis of mimesis, enchanting its prey by enacting a deep experiential 'I see me'/'me but not me' paradox.[2] This is why it captures animals with a peculiar disposition or attraction for self-knowledge. Exactly what sort of knowledge is that? With the help of ethnography, we shall travel into the forest and try to find out.

Technically, our aim in this chapter, like with the rest of the book, is to conduct an experiment in comparative philosophical anthropology. We invite the reader to approach this chapter as an opportunity to grow into a different understanding of the mirror: a hunting game of projection, participation, anticipation, mimicry and pretend. Hopefully, this will make for a 'captivating' story.

Captured: Traps as mirrors and mirrors as traps

We should start by talking a little more about traps. Perhaps even more important than understanding why mirrors can be seen to operate as traps is to see how traps often operate like mirrors. Traditional ethnographic accounts of hunting tell us that the use of traps is a common worldwide practice. From a functional point of view the making and setting of traps or snares is relatively simple. Yet, the idea of remote capture that those humble technologies embody is a complex one. Traps are more than smart hunting automata. The process of entrapment as a mode of material engagement and enactive signification, that is, a co-habitation through matter[3] between the hunter and the prey, can potentially expose relations of broader anthropological significance. The anthropologists Alberto Corsín Jiménez and Chloe Nahum-Claudel reviewing three major types of ethnographic narratives of trapping, namely, animistic, ecological and relational, propose that traps and notions of trapping can offer a useful anthropological heuristic for exploring the recursive entanglements of materiality, ecology and social life. The following eloquent description of trapping captures the heart of the matter:

> Traps are designed to mobilize, assemble and orient the circulation of energy in specific directions.... Bodies move in and out of traps, but it is not always clear whose body will be trapped and what exactly traps embody. Traps function thus as passageways for the circulation of 'endo- and exo-energies'.... They work as at once conductors and insulators of connectivity, accelerators and decelerators of mutuality or estrangement; as entrapments that body forth promissory but also dangerous worlds. (p. 15)[4]

Of course, no one has expressed better the semiotic complexity and metaphysical significance of traps than Alfred Gell, whose work we would like to quote here at some length. Gell's particular take on the agency of traps is guided by his radical anthropological reconceptualization of what art is and does that allow him a novel appreciation of traps as embodiments of complex intentionalities and thus, potentially artworks. Still, developing his case of traps as artworks and artworks as traps, he makes many valuable points of particular relevance to our own present concern to develop an argument of traps as mirrors and mirrors as traps.

Take an arrow trap from Africa. At a basic level, the trap operates by mere association and substitution. The arrow trap is a substitute of its creator; it becomes a surrogate hunter, translating into its material design its owner's hunting skills. Gell likens it to an 'automaton or robot'. The trap, he writes, is 'equipped with a rudimentary sensory transducer (the cord, sensitive to the animal's touch). This afferent nervous system brings information to the automaton's central processor (the trigger mechanism, a switch, the basis of all information-processing devices) which activates the efferent system, releasing the energy stored in the bow, which propels the arrows, which produce action-at-a-distance (the victim's death)'.[5]

Obviously, the association between the hunter and the trap that Gell is seeking to expose in the above description is not one based on mere visual similarity as with a doll that resembles a person. Instead, it is one based on translation where the trap provides a 'working model' for the hunter. We use the term 'translation' here to express the mentioned shift or delegation of the hunter's knowledge and skills into an artificial ensemble of organized matter, that is, the arrow trap, which can preserve and carry out the hunting task in his absence. Interestingly, not only the trap delegates the hunter, it also signifies the victim. In some cases, traps may simply 'reflect the outward form of the victim' or 'more subtly and abstractly, represent parameters of the animal's natural behaviour, which are subverted in order to entrap it'. Indeed, studying the form of a trap one could infer a great deal about the character and dispositions of the intended victim. 'In this sense', Gell continues, 'traps can be regarded as texts on animal behaviour. The trap is therefore both a model of its creator, the hunter, and a model of its victim, the prey animal. But more than this, the trap embodies a scenario, which is the dramatic nexus that binds these two protagonists together, and which aligns them in time and space'.[6]

Notwithstanding this entanglement between hunter and prey that the trap objectifies and mediates, there is also a semiotic double bind. To explain: on the one hand, the arrow trap, like all traps, is designed to be hidden. It can only fulfil its purpose if passed unnoticed. Traps are inherently secretive. They are not designed to communicate anything but 'a deadly absence – the absence of the man who devised and set it, and the absence of the animal who will become the victim'.[7] On the other hand, the arrow traps, like all traps, because of these marked absences, function as powerful enactive signs able to signify without speaking through their material structure: 'The static violence of the tensed bow, the congealed malevolence of the arrangement of sticks and cords, are revelatory in themselves, without recourse to conventionalization. Since this is a sign that is not, officially, a sign at all, it escapes all censorship. We read in it the mind of its author and the fate of its victim'.[8]

A trap, in its thoughtless cruelty, speaks the truth. An arrow trap indeed signifies the bloody scene which is to follow. It gives away its deadly intentions without shame or excuses. Another thing about traps is that they relate information about their creators and also about their future victims. As Alfred Gell neatly summarizes: 'Traps are lethal parodies of the animal's *Umwelt*'.[9] Seen as material signs, traps reveal the habits of their future prey as much as the needs and limits of the hunters. A trap always gives secrets away. It exposes the needs and weaknesses of its creator; it takes advantage of the anatomy and behaviour of prey, and paints a caricature of them both.

The mirror trap is just the same: it subtly points at the inabilities of its prey as well as of its creator. A human being, the mirror tells us, is not able of seeing oneself. We may be able to examine parts of our bodies – hands, feet, the front of our legs – but our face remains a mystery. The back of our bodies is out of reach. The mirror becomes, thus, our substitute eyes, like an arrow or a spear becomes a hunter's substitute hand. That is, the mirror becomes a prosthesis.[10] A technical alliance and alignment of materials, predictions, movements and life forms. It invites specific actions, fulfils intentions, reveals predispositions and entails anticipations. But how does it do it? What kind of energy the mirror trap stores and relays as the capture unfolds? The thing we should point out first is that the mirror trap embodies a visual ethos of care. It simultaneously reveals and conceals the victim's character traits, preferences, desires, beliefs and motives. Like any other trap, the presence of the mirror signifies an absence that binds the allure of mirroring with the victim's need. However, unlike other traps, the basic motive force that drives (or pulls) the victim to its entrapment is not pragmatic but rather epistemic. The human animal falls in the mirror trap not in order to feed its stomach but rather in order to fulfil a different kind of existential need. It is not hunger or the search for food but the animal's habitual quest for identity and self-knowledge that binds, aligns and entangles bodies and mirrors. The mirror is a trap we set for answers; it exhumes question marks: who we are, what we look like, how we appear in the eye of the other.

The knowledge of the self takes time and often comes at a great cost. The mirror trap works because its ingenious design tricks us to think that we can acquire that knowledge at a glance. So, the mirror works best for animals who want to know more. It serves our desire to make sense, to grasp the knowledge of our self. The problem is that what we recognize as 'our self' in front of the mirror is an intangible image made of light and glass that mimics our movement. The mirror image is elusive. It is simultaneously apparent and transparent, present and absent, self and other. Self-knowledge is hard to come by and almost impossible to possess entirely. Thus, self-awareness is not always guaranteed on the mirror's surface – coming to terms with our ever-changing image is not always successful: in our effort to capture and study our reflection sometimes we get entirely caught in the looking-glass.

To illustrate better our last point, we take a small detour. We visit Antoine Roquentin's room, the protagonist of Jean-Paul Sartre's famous novel *Nausea*.

Antoine is a young historian whose life seems utterly deprived of meaning. An illness creeps slowly on him interfering with his ability to define things; this inability sickens him. He feels nauseous. Antoine cannot even identify himself. His body, and the working of his body, seem to have become alienated. Desperate and alone, Antoine wishes for an 'iota of self-knowledge'[11] in order to make sense of the world. His lack of self-identification becomes unbearable. Eventually, on a cold Friday, Antoine is lured by the mirror:

> I get up. On the wall there is a white hole, the mirror. It is a trap. I know that I am going to let myself be caught in it. I have. The grey thing has just appeared in the mirror. I go over and look at it, I can no longer move away. It is the reflection of my face.[12]

Caught in the mirror trap Antoine is struggling to create some sort of personal narrative. He is not successful. The looking-glass reflects Antoine's characteristics, and yet, his reading of those signs leads him nowhere. The story he is supposed to make in front of the looking-glass – about who he is and what he looks like – fails, words escape him or seem irrelevant: 'I can understand nothing about this face', he admits.[13] The mirror reflects, for Antoine, a shapeless mass of flesh: 'My gaze travels slowly and wearily down over this forehead, these cheeks: it meets nothing firm, and sinks into the sand. Admittedly there is a nose there, two eyes and a mouth, but none of that has any significance, nor even human expression.'[14] Antoine pushes his face close to the mirror until it touches the glass. 'The eyes, the nose, the mouth disappear: nothing human is left ... Brown wrinkles on each side of the feverish swelling of the lips, cervices, mole-hills.'[15] The face is discredited, distorted and fragmented – unable to communicate personal identity. It is a face put to shame. Antoine wants to destroy it. The face is punished for its inability to form a person inside the mirror. Still, Antoine keeps returning in front of the looking-glass and keeps contemplating on his reflection. Despite of his repeated failures the promise of self-recognition pulls him back into the mirror trap. Is he ever successful? No, he is not. Instead of finally finding a self, Antoine's mirroring loses any trace of humanity. In fact, Antoine remembers the words of his aunt: '"If you look at yourself too long in the mirror, you'll see a monkey there." I must have looked longer than that: what I see is far below the monkey, on the edge of the vegetable world, at the polyp level.'[16]

Antoine's gaze generates a self which is unhitched from its mirrored reflection. That unhitched self is faceless. It drifts away aimlessly. The nauseous gaze would not co-operate with the mirror. The mirror throws that gaze back to Antoine's face: 'The eyes in particular, seen at such close quarters, are horrible. They are glassy, soft, blind, and red-rimmed; anyone would think they were fish scales.'[17] The eyes in the glass are alien to Antoine. They seem to belong more to the mirror than to him: blind, glass eyes; eyes incapable of producing vision. The 'blind' gaze is the mirror's answer to Antoine's misuse of it. It reflects Deleuze and Guattari's gazeless eyes[18] – a gaze out of focus, blank and nonsensical. It leads nowhere near self-assurance. It destroys the mirror. In a way, Antoine and mirror are at war. The notion of the self is the first casualty. The looking-glass eyes are barren and eerie: white globes 'on pink, bleeding flesh'.[19] But there is nothing new about them. The gaze's infertility becomes boring. Lulled by his monotonous and dreary reflection Antoine dozes off in front of the mirror. Unable either to escape the looking-glass or to make sense of his mirrored self, he gives away to sleep. Like an ensnared prey, Antoine's attitude changes from misapprehension and agony to surrender.

We borrow this story from Sartre's famous existential novel for two main reasons: first, because of what it reveals about the mirror trap and the role it has in the human existential struggle for self-specification. Second, because the story carries conviction whether you actually believe or not that Antoine Roquentin was a real person. As it is usually the case with traps, the mirror as an object makes no sense in the absence of the gaze of the prey: our gaze, which is drawn to it with a force we cannot always explain. We, the imaginary prey of mirrors, feel it clearly as an itch to step forth. Sartre describes that feeling perfectly through Antoine's existential drama that eventually leads him to fall into the 'white hole' of the mirror trap.[20]

The mirror is a subtle trap. It counts on us being smart – on our innate curiosity that compels us to gaze at our reflection and engage in the complex relationship of self and self-image. We are captured in the mirror not because we are naïve but because we are curious. Most of all, the reason we fall in the mirror trap is we do not see it as a trap; we do not feel anything like prey. Since the mirror trap does not involve poisonous arrows (at least not in the literal sense) we have the opportunity of countless glances. If the mirror is a trap, it is one we escape as many times as we fall in. And still, there is no way we could outsmart it. Gell offers us the example of a hippopotamus to illustrate the sense of false security that leads prey to its trap. Confident in his sheer strength and bulk, the hippopotamus disregards a rope blocking its way. The hunter, counting on that attitude, had the rope connected to a lethal device with a sharp pointy end hanging from the branch of a tree. The scenario embodied in the trap is easy to read: the hippopotamus will walk across in defiance, cut the rope and release the deadly device on its head. 'The fact that animals who fall victim to traps have always brought about their downfall by their own actions, their own complacent self-confidence, ensures that trapping is a far more poetic and tragic form of hunting than the simple chase.'[21]

A final point: Apart from any pronounced frame, the mirror is almost indistinguishable from its surroundings, albeit shinier. That is to say, in the manner of a trap camouflaging into its environment, the mirror excels. At some point though, the presence of the mirror's smooth, reflecting surface becomes clear. That is the moment when everything changes: the moment that we realize the absence. The looking-glass is 'empty'. Once we know that a mirror is placed close to us, the urge to move a little and see our face in it is almost tangible. There is a tension that lurks in an empty trap. Energy that begs to be spent, transformed or exchanged. Mirrors are waiting for us, empty and silent. Eventually, we'll fall into them. One way or another, we will be forced to confront our mirror self-image. That is the mirror's promise. Throughout development and human evolution the promise of self-identification has proven to be an irresistible bait. We are almost compelled to look in the mirror, as a mouse is compelled to get the cheese in the mouse trap. It is, however, hard to admit our entrapment. Rather, we resemble a victim that willingly lives its life inside a cage simply because the door is open. As it is, the mirror trap has come to feel like home.

Mimicry in the land of the 'soul hunters'

We have set out in this chapter to raise the question of how does a mirror relate to catching prey and to understand what kind of forces (mechanical, affective or semiotic) are involved or released during that process: How does the mirror trap work and what kind of work does it do? We have already made some progress with those questions by establishing in the previous section the conceptual foundation for our grounding metaphor of mirror as trap. We are now in need of a more practical hunting lesson. Anthropology has plenty to offer. For our first stop in our hunting exploration we choose to visit the land of the 'soul hunters', the Yukaghirs of Northeastern Siberia.[22] This is a place where hunters and prey mirror each other in unexpected ways. We want to follow those ways through the ethnography of Rane Willerslev and use them to understand some hidden dimensions of mirroring that perhaps will help us to answer our questions. For our second stop we visit two neighbouring groups in the equatorial rainforest of Amazonia: the Jivaros and the Tukanos. Our anthropological guide here is Philippe Descola's *Beyond Nature and Culture*.[23] In both cases we draw on the anthropological metaphysics of hunting, aiming to explore how different types of predation as well as issues of reciprocity and domination can help us understand better the central idea of the mirror as trap.

Before we embark into this didactic hunting excursion, a brief explanatory note is in order. It concerns our usual perception of the human–animal divide and ideas of personhood. To state in brief what lies at the heart of the matter we borrow the words of an elderly Yukaghir hunter: 'animals, trees, and rivers are "people like us"'.[24] In the land of the Yukaghirs, as is usually the case with other animist worlds, animals and people can borrow each other's form. For limited periods of time, animals can turn to people and people can turn into animals. Personhood is not an exclusively human trait. Persons may appear as rivers, trees or animals. Objects, animals and humans are all said to have an *ayibii*, a 'life essence' and the world is 'thus animated by living souls'.[25] To take on the appearance of an animal and adopt its viewpoint is, according to Rane Willerslev, one of the key characteristics of being a person. Non-human persons like the elk and the reindeer, the wolf, the bear, the fox and the raven see themselves as humans do; that is, living in human-like households along with their kin. A predatory animal, Willerslev states, will see a human as prey. For prey animals a human is viewed as a predator. Life is a matter of the soul, and the soul, the life essence, is equal in animals and humans. The perspective of a species depends on the bodies they 'wear'. In other worlds, one sees the world from a different viewpoint once in a changed body. Understanding the world becomes now mostly a bodily affair and depends on bodily functions.

But in this context, bodies are exchangeable. Since animals are persons, they have a will of their own; they have preferences.

The Yukaghir hunter is convinced that to kill a deer the deer must be fond of the hunter.

> [I]n the opinion of the Yukaghir, a lucky hunt depends on
> the good-will of the animal's guardian-spirit but also on
> that of the animal itself. Thus they say: '*tolo'w xanice
> e'rietum el kude'deti*' – that is: 'if the reindeer does not like
> the hunter, he will not be able to kill it'.[26]

Hunting is a lethal game of attraction in which the hunter, essentially, acts like a mirror: to be liked by a deer the hunter must mimic its species. He must disguise himself into a deer and imitate its movements. By doing so he is thought to adopt both the human perspective and the perspective of the animal. The Yukaghirs dress themselves in fur and wear masks and antlers to imitate the appearance of prey. They appear, basically, like the prey's mirrored reflection. Mimetic practice allows the hunter to become like the animal and both hunter and animal acquire mirroring points of view. Obviously, the limit between self and other, man and animal, is unclear. The hunter must simultaneously be one with himself (his human self) and the other (his prey) without forgetting who he was before the transformation started. It is therefore crucial for him to maintain his human point of view: he is the hunter who kills the animal and eats it. There is a danger in the metamorphosis of the hunter. By becoming the deer's mirroring, the hunter might lose himself completely. The Yukaghir hunters, therefore, struggle to transform their bodies into the image of the prey without losing human perspective.

To help us understand the danger of the hunter's metamorphosis to a mirror image of his prey, Willerslev tells a story of an old Yukaghir hunter who had been following a herd of reindeer: after about six hours on their track, the hunter developed a feeling of being watched. He then saw an old man a few meters away from him. The old man also took notice of the hunter and smiled. When the hunter talked to him, asking him who he was, the old man did not reply but only gestured to the hunter to follow him. The hunter was tired and hungry and thought that the old man was willing to share some food with him. So, the hunter followed the silent old man up the trail. Then, the hunter noticed something strange: the old man's footprints were those of a reindeer, even though he was wearing *kamus* (skin-covered) skis. But the hunter thought he was hallucinating because of exhaustion and hunger and paid no further attention to the animal marks. Eventually, the two men reached a big camp behind the hill. The camp was full of people, old and young. Children were running around, women were cooking food and men were sitting and smoking. The old man took the hunter to his tent. But when he spoke to his wife, his voice was not human: 'He spoke to his wife by grunting just like a reindeer, and she grunted back.'[27] The hunter was very confused. He had no memory of those people or their camp behind the hill. Yet, when the woman gave him a serving of moss, the hunter ate it and thought it tasted good. Time was passing and the hunter started forgetting things. He remembered he had a wife, and that his wife was waiting for him, but he could not recall her name. And when he fell asleep, he dreamt that he was surrounded by reindeer. Someone then spoke to the hunter and told him that he had no place there, that he must leave. The hunter woke up and knew he had to escape. He left the camp secretly and walked all the way back to his home. His presence seemed surprising to the people of his village, as if they never expected to see him again: 'They said they thought I had died. "What do you mean?" I asked them, "I have only been away for a week." "No," they said. 'We have not seen you for more than a month.'[28] Suddenly, the hunter realized what had happened to him: 'It seems that the people I met were reindeer, and I should have killed them, but at the time I did not know.'[29]

For the Yukaghir hunter, assuming the identity of the prey could lead to the loss of the self. Mimesis carries a risk. Through the mirroring act – the attempt to move, look and even smell like a reindeer or an elk – a hunter may lose his sense of selfhood. He may become completely alienated from humankind and remain forever a prisoner in the world of the prey. The hunter of the above story, Willerslev suggests, instead of deceiving the reindeer by disguising himself like one, was himself tricked by the animal. He believed he was one of them – a member of the reindeer herd. Therefore, he saw the world through the eyes of a reindeer, lived in their community, ate their food and in this dangerous game of double identities he almost lost himself completely. The hunter, one might say, fell for his own sham: he fell into his mimetic trap. Misled by a false image the hunter lost his self-identity and turned to prey. In the Yukaghir hunting world of seductive mirroring, both hunter and prey are in danger.

Stories of transformation

We now return to our discussion of the mirror trap. We want to ask an important question that may seem misleadingly simple: in the vicinity of the mirror trap who exactly is the hunter and who/what is the prey? Obviously, human beings are making the mirrors and placing them into their surroundings with their own hands. In that respect, it is legitimate to assume that humans – the creators of the trap – are the hunters. As humans, at least in our modern version, we like to claim that we are in control of the mirror as much as we are of everything else we create. But then, the mirror trap is set for humans to be caught in it. We set the trap for us to fall. Clearly, the mirror is a trap like no other: a trap to catch an image. On a fundamental level, we construct and use a mirror to capture images of ourselves, to tame the inevitable uncertainties of who and what we are. The mirror is our prime weapon for self-hunting. A weapon that operates as a material sign based on the principles of mimesis. The problem is that, as with Yukaghirs' hunting mimicry, mirror hunting involves many dangers: like the Yukaghir hunter tricked into believing he was actually the animal whose image he impersonated, we might come to suppose that we are one with our mirror reflection. In contemporary societies that prefer to trade on representations and images, the threat is more pronounced. The mirror image poses an existential threat to the living body.

The Yukaghirs emphasize the risk involved in travelling between one's real body and an alien one, that is, the journey between real body and deer. They associate that journey with feelings of profound anxiety and self-loss. Willerslev reports an experience of deep-anxiety and self-alienation – a loss of one's sense of personhood. 'Thus, an element of self-awareness or reflexivity is crucial to safeguarding oneself against being carried away by an alien body.'[30] In the case of the mirror, the 'alien body' is not a body at all but the reflection of the body. And yet, we need a similar sense of self-awareness because we embark on a similar journey: the journey between felt body and mirroring – an ongoing, everyday visual drama. A sense of dislocation and self-alienation is innate in mirror gazing. Maintaining our human point of view in front of our mirrored self is as crucial for us as it is for the disguised Yukaghir hunter mimicking the deer. Not because we do not understand that what we are viewing is just an image, but because our tendency is to misconstrue the self-image for all that matters. The following remark on photography by the writer and film-maker Susan Sontag may be relevant here: the true trait of modernity, she writes, is not to regard the image as 'the real thing', photographic images are hardly that real. Instead reality has come to seem more and more like what we are shown by cameras'.[31] A similar representational ontology operates in the case of mirror gazing. Of course, unlike the members of the Biami tribe discussed in Chapter 2, the mirroring rarely surprises or scares us. Our eyes are far from innocent. And yet, in our image-obsessed society the mirrored self trespasses the borders of the real. It becomes the real 'us' in the eye of the other and in social media. It becomes, thus, troublesome.

The aim is therefore the same: the Yukaghir hunters should not forget who they were before they became the victim's mirroring, and we must not forget who we were before we gazed in the mirror and turned into a mirroring of ourselves. Otherwise, we might fall into the mirror trap and become the image we gaze at. Not, of course, in a literary sense, but in the way we understand, think about and evaluate ourselves. As a physical reality, the mirror face in the looking-glass can easily be accounted for as a simple, inanimate reflection. But the experience of our mirror face poses a different challenge because it carries with it our aspirations and fears concerning our image, social stereotypes and demands. With no other means to visually apprehend ourselves, our mirror image becomes the self of our imagination and at the same time society's puppet. A hybrid 'creature', half the product of our own making, that is, of the phenomenal 'I' that perceives and experiences the world from the inside, and half the product of our social environment, that is, the 'other' that always gazes us from the outside. The topology we have used to conceptualize this relationship, 'inside' and 'outside', is usually misleading when it comes to understanding self-becoming. But in the case of the mirror it offers a useful way to describe the phenomenological tension involved between the experience of looking at our self in the mirror and that of conceptualizing our self through the mirror. Blending mimesis with alterity, the outer with the inner, the mirroring is gesturing to us silently to follow it, like the deer gestured at the hunter deep in the forests of the Yukaghirs. If we do follow it, we enter a domain where the real body transforms into an image which transforms into reality. Such being the case, instead of finding our self in the mirror, we lose it completely in naive deception.

Willerslev, in his ethnography, describes a personal experience of self-transformation while hunting sable with a young Sakha man from Nelemnoye of Siberia. Both worked very hard and indeed managed to catch many sables. Nevertheless, Willerslev writes, the two men became obsessed with setting traps and accumulating furs. They neglected their need for rest, firewood and even food.

> We always fell asleep in a cold cabin, exhausted and hungry. Then one evening, when we were lying side by side on our plank bed, my companion said: 'Can't you feel it?' 'Feel what?' I asked. 'How we are turning into greedy predators, just like wolves. We have this need to kill more and more. Even if we had two hundred sables we wouldn't feel satisfied, would we? Just like the devil, you see'. He paused for a while. Then he added, 'I suggest we calm down (Russian: *uspokoit'sya*) and stop hunting for a week or so'.[32]

Unlike hunting reindeer or elk, trapping does not involve disguising into the animal by moving, smelling or sounding like them, but a need to think like the animal. To set traps for sable, a hunter does not have to imitate their appearance. Yet, it involves the ability to attain and to internalize the animal's point of view. The danger of the loss of the hunter's sense of personhood is again present: thinking like a sable a hunter may develop the animal's blood lust. The sable's greed for blood equals that of a fox's and a wolf's, and this is why those animals are called 'children of the devil' by the locals. A hunter who loses his human point of view to become like them is called the 'devil's son' and is equally careless. Such a hunter would experience only the present, like the animals, and would know no past or future.

Yukaghir myths are full of stories of transformation where different species take on each other's bodies. Many of those stories involve members of a giant cannibal tribe, *cou'liye*, who turn into handsome men to seduce Yukaghir girls and eat them.[33] The giants call their victims 'elk' or 'reindeer' as to them human beings are animal prey. In some stories, however, the cannibalistic non-humans fall in love with their intended victims and abandon their own communities. In such a story, a young cannibal giant marries the Yukaghir girl he was supposed to eat and lives among her kin. Yet, the transformation cannot completely erase the desire for human flesh. One time, as he is in bed with his wife, the transformed giant says to her while touching her breast: "'My late father used to feed me with such things".[34] The wife gets worried and tells the rest of the camp about the episode. The people agree that the former cannibal is not entirely transformed and so they kill him.' The situation is confusing: the Yukaghirs, by killing the husband, murdered a transformed cannibal but also one of their own. In killing a relative they have committed an unforgivable sin. As a result, the 'Sun deity' punished the Yukaghirs by taking their fire away and letting them all freeze to death.[35]

To take on the body of another is complicated. The new body might deceive and seduce, but it is not easily controlled. The giant cannibal tamed his true nature enough to marry the girl he loved but could not escape the memories of tasting human flesh. The humans who killed him, however, were punished since the deity who judged them obviously recognized the transformation of the giant as real. To demonstrate further the complications and consequences of transformation, Willerslev cites another story involving two girls seeking revenge on the man who killed their parents. The man was called Lower Jaw and, to kill him, the girls transformed themselves into wolves. To achieve the transformation, the girls simply went down on their hands and knees and started to move around like wolves. After turning into predators and killing the man and his son, the wolf-girls ate their victims. Normally, Willerslev suggests, cannibalism is seen as a terrible crime by the Yukaghirs, and it is punished. But at the time the two girls ate their victims they had taken on the bodies of wolves and, therefore, they subscribed to the moral code of those predators. Wolves, naturally, are allowed to eat human flesh. So, the girls were not punished but took on their human form again and lived a normal life among their people. What we learn from the story is that, for the Yukaghirs, once a person transforms into the image of an alien body, it is the new body that determines the person's point of view. Humans are not responsible for their actions while in transformation. The new body claims the soul.

The mirror image presents us with a different point of view: it transforms us into what we believe other people see of us, it turns us into objects.

Through the mirroring we identify with a 'new body': a traceless body. Then, we think with it. Could it be that the mirroring claims some of our *ayibii*, our 'life essence' as its own? It certainly moves and looks like us. It appears somewhat alive. In that sense, the mirroring is a cannibalistic image: it feeds from us. There is always the danger of 'sharing' our life with it; of letting it 'steal' something of our humanity. The acceptance, promotion and circulation of the mirrored self – the mirror selfie distributed in social media is a good example here – results in the social marginalization of the physical self. It is a looting of the living body for which the 'new body' cannot be blamed. Why? Because the mirrored self lacks responsibility: like a Yukaghir temporarily transformed into a wolf it abides to a different moral code – that of the new social and visual media. The 'new body' develops a ceaseless thirst for attention. It lives for the moment. It constantly needs approval. It is forever seeking proof of existence. It leads a life of no consequence. Losing our human point of view in our everyday hunt for a perfect digital self might mean adopting the behaviour of an image.

Do we still have the upper hand? Undoubtedly, the mirroring is totally dependent on us, but, since we rely on it for self-awareness and to construct, assume and communicate a social self that otherwise never existed, our own autonomy has been compromised. Self and mirrored self are now living parallel lives.

Seducing Narcissus

How many times, in vain, he leans to kiss
The pool's deceptive surface or to plunge
His arms into water, keen to clasp
The neck he glimpses but cannot embrace ...

Ovid, *Metamorphoses, Book III*

The mirroring is an image capable of producing multiple and opposite effects. At the start of this chapter we briefly discussed the self-rejecting gaze of Antoine Roquentin, the protagonist of Jean-Paul Sartre's famous novel *Nausea*. Now we take another detour, this time in Greek mythology, where we trace a mirroring so enticing it drives a young man to his death. The story is that of Narcissus, son of nymph Liriope and river god Cephisus. There are many versions of the Narcissus's myth. In Ovid's *Metamorphoses* we find a classic version[36]: Narcissus grows up to become a young man of astonishing beauty. His nymph mother asks Tiresias if her handsome boy will live to reach old age. Tiresias presents Liriope with a riddle: 'If he knows himself – not.'[37] By the time he is sixteen, Narcissus is loved and desired by anyone who sees him, male or female, but does not love anyone back. He is proud, distant and rejects anyone who tries to approach him. One day, a scorned lover asks for him to be punished for his callousness, and Nemesis, the Greek goddess of revenge, obliges.

Narcissus finds himself near a lake with pure water, undisturbed by humans or animals. On that lake's clear surface Narcissus sees his reflection perfectly for the first time. And for the first time in his life Narcissus is in love. Narcissus is 'overcome by the beauty of the image that he sees; he falls in love with an immaterial hope, a shadow that he wrongly takes for substance'.[38] The external world plays a malevolent trick at him: like a hunter the lake 'disguises' as Narcissus, and Narcissus does not immediately realize that what he is looking at is his mirrored face. He takes his reflection to be that of another and that other seems magnificent – an ideal and willing lover. A fatal attraction begins. Narcissus encounters his image and is beguiled by it: 'Transfixed, suspended like a figure carved from marble, he looks down at his own face; stretched out on the ground.'[39]

The confusion between self and image is one that Narcissus is unable to overcome. In vain Ovid warns Narcissus of the illusion: 'Child, what you seek is nowhere to be found, your beloved is lost when you avert your eyes: that image of an image without substance, arrives with you and with you it remains, and it will leave when you leave – if you can.'[40] But he can't. Young Narcissus is unable to turn his back on his self-reflection. The desire, the need, for his mirroring is stronger than his love for his real physical self. Even when Narcissus realizes that what he has been looking at all this time is his own reflection, the spell is not broken. The seduction of the perfect mirroring proves lethal. Narcissus remains tied down to his image, obsessed by it.

In front of the mirror, the void that separates body and reflection, disguised hunter and enticed prey, is overcome by a stubborn illusion: we are here and we are also there. The mirror image captures the body by modifying its physicality into something fictional. 'In other words, the body is not the body. Its construction has been transposed into the domain of the image; the body which we inhabit is indissociable from the grip of the image.'[41] Narcissus bestows to his mirrored self a value which is untranslatable into real experience. The lake turns into a flawless mirror trap and the young man, seduced by his mirroring, is unable to move away.

Narcissus believes his mirrored self to be the most beautiful and captivating thing he had ever seen. Truly, if Antoine Roquentin from Sartre's *Nausea* finds nothing beautiful or even human in the mirror, Narcissus finds everything: eyes that look like 'a pair of stars worthy of Bacchus, a head of hair that might adorn Apollo; those beardless cheeks, that neck of ivory, the decorative beauty of his face, and the blushing snow of his complexion.'[42] Narcissus mirrored face is irresistible.

Narcissus's gaze is an addiction: it is how a victim encounters the mirror. His gaze 'an insatiate stare fixed on that false shape'[43] is the gaze of the deer looking at the enchanting image of the Yukaghir hunter: the false shape of the man who pretends to be the animal's mirror image. Above all, Narcissus's gaze is a gaze that fails to be averted: a narcotic gaze. Narcissus's fatal flow is his inability to take his eyes away from his mirroring; he desires something which is his but could never have it. The empty adoration of one's own self generates a reflection of absolute poverty: 'Why seek at all, when all that I desire is mine already? Riches in such abundance that I've been left without means!'[44]

The reflecting water forms for Narcissus a death trap. It gives to the young man the means to gaze upon his own face but, whatever it grants to vision, Narcissus cannot handle the gift. The reflected eyes seem like twin stars but are essentially blinded by his predatorily aggression. The predatory character of self-reflection is revealed as it holds Narcissus there, desperate and helpless, ensnared in his own gaze. Narcissus fades away 'as the golden wax melts when it's warmed, or as the morning frost retreats before the early sun's scant heat'. [45] The heartbroken youth fell into the callous grip of self-adoration. Obsessed with his image and a future sexual promise, Narcissus abandons himself at the mercy of grief and unrequited love. More and more, the physical body is forsaken for the sake of its own mirroring. In the end, failing to escape, Narcissus ultimately dies in the mirror trap. Like the deer who gives itself up willingly for the love of the disguised hunter, Narcissus offers himself as prey to his likeness.

Hunter's beauty/the prey is in love

The Yukaghir hunter tricks the prey using its own image. The image becomes the hunter's weapon: it seduces and eventually draws the victim to its death. To become an elk's mirroring, apart from antlers and fur, the hunter wears skis with the smooth skin of an elk's leg to imitate the sound of the animal walking on snow. In the hunter's mimesis, the prey will see its own mirroring. Hunter and animal will get closer to each other – the hunter continuously imitating the movements of the prey as a huge mirror set up in the middle of the forest.

Mimesis influences the way one perceives and manipulates the surrounding world. According to Michael Taussig, the mimetic modes of perception lie at the basis of sympathetic magic.[46] Mimesis can bridge the distance between the self and the other (human on non-human). To mimic something is to be able to feel it outside one's body, to surrender to it and at the same time to control it. Here Taussig is influenced by Walter Benjamin's famous essay 'On the Mimetic Faculty', originally written in 1933, where he argues that the faculty of mimesis understood as an attempt to copy the 'outside' of the 'Other', but also a means of usurping its power, as well as of appropriating its meaning, is a universal feature of the human condition. When we mirror something bodily, the boundary between self and other, nature and culture, real and imagined, collapses.[47] Between hunter and prey develops a mimetic bond which is almost erotic. It does not happen quickly. The hunters' impersonation of the prey is 'a long process of opening their bodies',[48] which starts many days before the hunt. The hunters try to lose their human smell by the use of sauna and adopt a special linguistic code instead of ordinary human speech. When talking of their indented prey, they will never reveal its name: instead of 'elk' they might say 'the big one'. They will avoid uttering the word 'hunting', using in its place a phrase like 'going for a walk in the forest'. The hunters will never say 'kill'. Knives will not sharpen in the open revealing their intentions. Otherwise, the process of seduction will fail.

In that respect, the mirror is the perfect seducer: unlike a Yukaghir, or any other hunter on earth, it has no self to maintain, no form to lose, no smell to be rid of, no language to alter. It reflects our forms effortlessly; it becomes us. At some level this game of mimesis can be a source of pleasure. In the case of the Yukaghirs the pleasure is sexual. This is evident in the steps they take the nights before the hunting. The hunter's purpose here is to seduce the guardian spirits of animals to act in his favour. For this purpose, they cast exotic goods like vodka and tobacco into the fire to get the spirits into an erotic mood. Also, a drunken spirit will not recognize the hunter's disguise. It will fall for the false image and go to bed with him. The idea is that the emotions of lust and sexual pleasure will be extended from the guardian spirit to its physical counterpart which is the prey. And the next morning the animal will be besotted with the hunter. It will recall the love making and run towards him in sexual excitement. The hunter then will shoot it dead. In his sleep, therefore, the hunter will attempt to enter into the world of the shadows and reach the animal's guardian spirit and make love to it. Here are two examples of such nocturnal dream adventures. The first story is told by a middle-aged male hunter:

> They live in a wooden house. There is a barn too. I assume they keep the animals in the barn. They are always glad to see me, the three sisters. When I arrive, they are a little drunk [presumably, he is referring to the vodka offered when feeding the fire]. They start to play around with my penis. ... If I'm hunting at the upper part of the river, I'll take the oldest sister and we'll go to bed. If I hunt at the middle part, I'll pick the middle sister. And if I'm hunting at the lower part I'll go with the youngest one. When I wake up I know that in this season I will have good luck [in hunting].[49]

The second story is offered by an old woman:

> I was lying sleeping with my husband in the tent, when I suddenly heard a male voice calling me. 'Stand up', it said. I stood up. 'Go up the river', the voice said. It was as if I started flying up the river. 'Turn left', the voice said. I flew left, and there, in between the trees, stood a huge penis. (laughter) ... I won't tell you anymore. But next morning, when we got up, I said to my husband that I had had a dream. I didn't tell him what I had dreamt, but just said that we should go up river and then go to the left. So we did, and there, at the very same spot, stood a huge bull [elk] that my husband killed.[50]

After having tried his best in his sleep, the hunter will continue with his act of seduction when, in the morning, he will transform his body into the victim's image and go for the kill. The hunter would do his best to be handsome. His clothing fur will be immaculate, his ammunition belt colourful, his knife ornamented. Let's not forget: a victim is, above all, in love with itself.

Predatory image

Hunting, for the Yukaghirs, is a game of seduction and transformation. It depends on the narcissistic tendencies of the potential prey. But it is also a game of love and participation akin to sympathetic magic. The hunter's act to modify his body to resemble the victim invokes to the future prey feelings of empathy. Because of this empathy, the victim abandons its universe. The hunter transforms the victim's 'perception of reality into a manipulated fiction, which he then deliberately uses to kill it'.[51] The fiction: the hunter is a harmless lover. The victim will come to like not the hunter but its disguise. The hunter must remain unaffected and not surrender to feelings of love for the prey because love could lead to a real transformation: to the hunter actually becoming the prey. Love and seduction are two different things. Seduction is, according to Willerslev, to pretend love on the part of the hunter and vanity on the part of the seduced victim. Sometimes, however, a hunter gets absorbed in his mirroring act and forgets about the hunting. The victim gets away. The Yukaghirs claim that the reason for the escape was that the hunter fell in love with it. As a result, the hunter could start neglecting himself, stop eating and eventually die consumed by the love for his prey. In a case like that the soul of the hunter will be reincarnated as an animal and live among the prey. That is why, the Yukaghirs believe, some animals demonstrate strange behaviour and sometimes seek human company. If a deer or an elk comes too close to humans it might be that the animal has a human soul: the soul of a hunter that died in a mimicry act that went wrong.

The mirror image, on the other hand, is never in such danger. Narcissus's reflection would forever remain indifferent and elusive on the lake's cold water. Unlike a hunter who disguises himself into the image of an animal, the mirroring has no self to be transformed by real love. A mirrored reflection could never become like us, one of us, a credible part of any human self. Love for one's own image, therefore, can only pretend love: a common play of seduction and vanity – seduction on the part of the mirroring, vanity on the part of the mirror's observer.

The mirroring is an image ahead of its game. Its relationship with us is predatory. It plays on the observers' narcissistic inclinations. It manipulates one's perception. It can lead to self-absorption. It can even excite one to the point of self-surrender. The eyes of the deer, as they watch a hunter impersonating its image, stare at the soul of our story. Without those two eyes the nature of the mirroring would have been indescribable. The parallelism also serves an additional purpose. It allows us to ask our next question: what exactly do we surrender for the sake of our image? Working towards a possible answer in the last part of this chapter, we continue our discourse on the metaphysics of hunting by comparing two neighbouring groups in the equatorial rainforest of Amazonia drawing on Philippe Descola's *Beyond Nature and Culture*.[52] These are the Jivaros and the Tukanos.

Soul exchange in Amazonia

The Jivaros and the Tukanos of Colombian Amazonia live in small residential units close to each other (situated no more than a few hundred kilometres away). Their spatial proximity means that they share and live in similar environments. The equatorial rainforest offers pretty much the same resources and imposes similar ecological constraints upon both groups. They engage in hunting and fishing. They also cultivate manioc (sweet in the case of Tukanos, bitter in the case of Jivaros). The way they see and make sense of their environment is also similar. Like most Indians of Amazonia, both groups participate in what has been described as an 'animist ontology'. The distinctive feature of such a world view is that humans, animals and plants, regardless of their differences in physicality, are thought to maintain a similar social and ceremonial life. Such a perspectivist ontology is predicated on the continuity of soul or selfhood and the discontinuity of body.[53] This is not just to say that humans maintain personal relations and alliances with plants, animals and the spirits they protect them. Rather, it means that in sharing some of the ontological attributes of the humans with whom they form a network of exchange many plants and animals are regarded as persons. Both groups, Descola informs us, 'categorize humans, plants and animals as "people" (*masa*, in the Tukano languages) or as "persons" (*aents* in the Jivaro languages) all of whom possess an analogous interiority'. To put it simply, within such an animistic and participatory world, humans can maintain with plants, animals and spirits the same kind of social relations that we see among the Indians themselves. Exchange is at the heart of social relationships in Amazonia – if not everywhere. 'Everything seems to circulate in an unending round of reciprocity', Descola observes referring to the ethnographic legacy of Claude Lévi-Strauss in the lowlands of South America.[54] Marriageable women, goods and the dead are exchanged between men. Plants, foods and animals are exchanged between women. Hunters exchange offerings to the animals they hunt in return for their meat.

Yet, despite sharing a world of similar ecological and ontological constraints, the Jivaros and the Tukanos seem to have a very different attitude towards their obligations and responsibilities. As Descola writes, although both groups 'conceive of their relations with animals as being governed by relations of affinity, the content that they ascribe to those relations could not be more different. Whereas the Jivaro hunter treats his prey as a brother-in-law who is potentially hostile and to whom nothing is owed, the Desana hunter treats it as a spouse whose line of descent he is fertilizing.'[55] In the former case of the Jivaros their hostility towards the prey leads them to avoid their obligations of exchange. By contrast, the Tukanos aim to honour their obligations governed by a general principle of reciprocal dependence in their interaction with the fellow inhabitants of their cosmos. To understand the relevance and importance of that difference, we need to understand the role that exchange and reciprocity plays in both groups and how it defines their relationship with other people (human and non-human).

Let's take a closer look at both groups starting with the Jivaro.

The different Jivaro tribes are in a constant warfare. Descola believes that one reason Jivaros fight is to maintain self-continuity. To retain a sense of continuity, they must take parts of other people's identities. Headhunting provides the Jivaros the means to take those elements without having to reciprocate. Headhunting means taking the head of an enemy and shrinking it. The shrinking takes place as part of a long and elaborate ritual. Its purpose is mainly to remove the identity of the dead person and then transfer that identity to the group of the murderer. In this way a virtual person is created. This newly acquired identity would compensate for deaths within the kindred group and become the principle for the birth of a new child. It will allow the victor or his kin to multiply without having to oblige to marital reciprocity. Still, through ritual, the *tsantsa*, the final product of the severed head after desiccating and the modelling of its characteristics, is not to be a miniature of its former owner. The *tsantsa* is, above all, an opportunity for a new person to come into existence. The sole and most important function is for it to act, in Descola's words, as an identity you can transport, a pure individuality. For the *tsantsa* to maintain a resemblance with the victim is not problematic. Personal identity is not preserved in facial features but by other social traits like name, speech, memory, face paintings and shared experiences. The Jivaro, however, take certain precautions in order to make sure that the *tsantsa* is free of any traces of past identity: they never call the *tsantsa* by the name of the person it used to belong to; all the head's orifices are sewn up thus provoking to the sense organs an amnesia which is phenomenal and external, and, finally, the head is blackened to obliterate the memory that resides in the patterns painted on it.

During the year-long *tsantsa* ritual, the head is known as many things and is called by many names: soft thing, giver of women, wife, and at the last stage, embryo. Once the ritual is completed, a baby can be born within the murderer's group without commitments or requirements. The baby is, in a sense, the real outcome of all that simulated alliance and owns its existence to an ideal affinity. The only affinity, Descola claims, truly desired by the Jivaros: that which is free of any reciprocity, an affinity 'devoid of affines'. Descola also mentions vendetta warfare which may not involve the capturing of heads but evolve around the same principle of the predatory taking of the dead man's belongings. The wives of the defeated enemy now belong to the victor and any young children are adopted and raised as his own. The end goal is again the same: the enlargement of one's family without the necessary obligations of reciprocity that a proper marriage alliance would entail. Very simply, the Jivaros dislike giving things back for what they take. Their relationship with their cosmos is predatory and killing is the essence of it, the stuff to build one's community on. The world is something you grab, not share. Identity is forged through warfare. Adolescent boys must contact an 'arutam' spirit to form a relationship with the ghost of a dead Jivaro warrior who will provide him with bravery and protection. Yet, the assistance and courage a terrifying 'arutam' spirit unleashes upon the young warrior will fade with the murder of each enemy. The warrior is then left vulnerable and weak. Personal strength is something to be renewed constantly. Therefore, his whole existence is bound to an endless circle of violence. This predatory attitude, the need to constantly incorporate, according to Descola, the bodies and identities of other people in order to maintain a self, means that the Jivaros are defined by what they kill and assimilate. It is also a prevailing attitude in the relation of the Jivaros with animals: seizure is preferred over established reciprocity.

The predatory ideology is also extended to plants. It rules relationships even when killing is not directly involved. Manioc, the most common plant in the Jivaro diet, is believed to be able to kill. It sucks the blood of people that touches its leaves. Most often it attacks the women who take care of it and their children. Sometimes, the Jivaro accuses the plant for the death of a baby. Manioc's vampirism would be brought to discussion and the death would be attributed to anaemia. Women sing to plants to divert their blood thirst away from themselves or their children and direct it towards less loved relatives. The manioc plant, it seems, is a child, but one that would be eventually eaten by the family. At the same time, the manioc tries to kill the human children who brush by its leaves. Nothing is benign. Even gardening entails, as Descola describes, a lethal tension – an aggressive relationship between human and non-human children out to eat each other. Women should cultivate the plant-children whose flesh will become porridge for their human-children and they must do so while preventing the cannibalistic plant from avenging the family by sucking their blood. From the capturing of heads to the hunting of animals and the cultivation of the manioc plant, the Jivaros experience a world of predatory tension.

Now, let's turn our attention to the Tukanos of Colombian Amazonia, the group that Descola cites as a counter-example to the Jivaros. We start with the Desana, one of the many Tukano groups. Descola points out their belief that an omnipotent creature, the Father Sun, created the world with its fertilizing energy. The energy must be exchanged between the different inhabitants of the cosmos, and, because it is not infinite, it must be re-directed into the close circuit that engulfs the biosphere. For hunting, this means that every time an animal is killed part of this energy passes to the human sphere and is cut off from the animal domain. Consequently, the hunter must ensure that they kill only what is needed for their survival and nothing more, so the circulation of energy won't be imperilled. The hunter is there to guard the energy flow. For animals to be hunted and killed human souls are offered in return. That means that the souls of the Desana who, in life, disrespected the rules of exchange will become animals to compensate for the energy loss. Shamans also negotiate the exchange between humans and animals by communicating with animal's spirit-masters. A human whose soul will eventually become an animal must be available for every forest animal that will be killed: souls in return for game, the principle process of energy feedback that Descola called *the traffic of souls*. Therefore, humans and animals are equals. They have equal access to energy and both strive to preserve the harmony of its flow.

Animals and humans accept freely the importance of equality and fair exchange among each other. Hunters regenerate those they destroy: they chant incantations before they eat an animal, ensuring that its spirit will find its way back to its house and be reborn. There is an understanding of mutual dependence between humans and animals and all action is governed by egalitarian exchange. The soul exchange, the negotiation and offering of a human soul in place of animal ensures not only that hunting will continue to be successful but also that excesses will be prevented. Overkill is thought to be punished. A hunter's hubris will be avenged in the forest by a fatal accident. The symmetry of obligation and the harmony of the energy flow are not negotiable. Upon them depends the survival of the world.

This is symmetry in the forest: a constant negotiation between hunter and prey to prevent overindulgence. The hunter, in engaging with the world, takes care not to exhaust his relationship with it. So, what we take here is a lesson in symbiosis, in existing together without wearing each other out. We learn that a hunter may trap one hundred animals, but chooses that he can only have two.

Hunters and prey: The gaze of the prey

We started this book with the image of a deer standing in front of a mirror. We said that some of the strangest, but also interesting, things in human life can be understood as relations between hunters and prey. In this chapter, adopting the metaphor of the mirror as trap, we have tried to situate and explore the logic of mirroring (in its broader sense) within the relevant anthropological discussion of the complex relations between hunters and prey. We have argued that humans can approach and engage with the mirror both as hunters and prey. All living creatures are potentially prey of one form or another; only few of them will ever become hunters. Being a prey is natural. Being a hunter demands skill.

We may think of certain animals as natural predators. But a predator is not a hunter. An act of predation is essentially about location, mutilation and destruction of prey. An act of hunting, by contrast, is dialogical and participatory. It is a social act. A predator primarily kills; a hunter, by contrast, collects, relates and participates. This is why becoming a hunter presupposes the ability to become a prey: the two roles are inseparable, their relationship is one of reciprocity, alliance and sympathy. As we saw for the hunter of the Siberian forest the very act of hunting, of killing, is based on mimicry and is governed by the kind of affective logic we've seen in the case of erotic alliances among human partners. A similar symmetric alliance can be seen in the case of the Tukanos tribes where animals and humans accept freely the importance of equality and fair exchange among each other. On the contrary, a predator, like the Amazonian Jivaros, never really knows what it is like to be prey. Even though the hunted animals are considered to be persons (described according to gender like brother-in-law or potential wife) they are not given anything in exchange for their bodies. The tone is that of a forced affability. The Jivaros' intention is not to share or to form an alliance with the animals but to fool them so that they will not escape their killing arrows or punish them for their cannibalistic intentions.

The reason we have chosen the above ethnographic examples for this comparative study is because they provide us with an interesting complication of the question about what it means to adopt the perspective of the hunter, instead of prey, in front of the mirror. Those examples also help us to understand the important differences between a hunter and a predator. The predator consumes, the hunter exchanges. The hunter must reciprocate in one form or another for being allowed to receive the benefits of food. By contrast, the predator feels no obligation to offering anything in exchange. In the latter sense killing is asymmetrical, and in the former symmetrical and participatory. We are not saying that a hunter is not going to kill the prey very much like the predator does. But killing in the animist contexts of hunting is different: it can also be viewed as an act of benevolence. The act of killing is just an appearance for what Descola describes as a gift: 'It is always out of a feeling of generosity that a hunted animal delivers itself up to the hunter. Moved by compassion for humans in the grip of hunger, it presents him with its carnal envelope, as a gift, without expecting any compensation.'[56] The contrasting examples of the Amazonian Tukanos and Jivaros make an interesting case, precisely because of what they can teach us about the different ways by which the hunting for self-identity can be responsive and attentive, or unresponsive and inconsiderate to the suffering of 'others'. We have seen two neighbour ontologies of hunting, one that permits participatory exchange (the Tukanos) and one which does not (the Jivaros).

Perhaps, all that may seem far removed from our contemporary habits of mirror gazing. The logic of our comparison may become clearer if we remind ourselves the central idea of this chapter, that is, the mirror as trap. During our everyday engagement with our mirror self-image, we constantly adopt and exchange the above roles, that is, we can be the hunter, the predator, but also the prey. Not only the mirror has the potential to capture the self-image we see in it, it has become all the more evident that we can't get enough of it. 'A capitalistic society', Susan Sontag's remarks, feeds on images, 'in order to stimulate buying and anaesthetise the injuries of class, race, and sex. … The freedom to consume a plurality of images and goods is equated with freedom itself. The narrowing of free political choice to free economic consumption requires the unlimited production and consumption of images.'[57] Increasingly in our days, the image most fervently produced and consumed is the self-image. In social media we put our self-images on display. Our mirrored bodies become public spectacle while countless self-images (selfies, mirror-selfies, etc.) are offered for consumption to fellow image-consumers. Consuming, of course, is devouring – building up a need for more. So, very quickly, new images must be produced to replace the 'devoured' ones. To keep up with the production of self-images we keep on glancing in the mirror, in our smartphones screen or use the mirror app which turns our phones and tablets into functional mirrors, searching for that next mirroring we are going to share with the world. 'The management of image and self-image is an undeniably dominant contemporary compulsion.'[58] We want to control the images with which we fuel social media and consequently sketch a social self. But could our mirror gaze ever be satisfied?

The relationship between self and mirrored self becomes greedy, burdened and aggressive, in some sense cannibalistic: like the Jivaro's manioc plant that feeds the family and, at the same time, is thought to suck the blood out of them, the mirror image might feed our ego but might also consume us. Instead of symbiotic, our relationship with the mirror is now predatory.[59] Take for instance our contemporary practices of digital mirroring using selfies. In a way, a Jivaro needs to maintain his identity in his forest with constant acts of reassurance like we do in the world of social media through constantly posting images of our self. The selfie becomes obsolete the minute it is created and generates the need for the production of the next one to reaffirm our identity and re-establish our image in the surrounding world of digital images. The relentless struggle to renew energy and identity communicates a tension that is, in both cases, predatory. The mirror image captured in our smartphone takes up all space, becoming our new environment. We linger, voluntarily inside a mirroring, in a digital Plato's cave of the twenty-first century.

As we saw, Willerslev describes the Yukaghir hunter's mimicking act as a process of sexual seduction. The seduction depends on the prey becoming fascinated by its own image. The hunter, therefore, should disguise himself to become not an exact image of the prey, but an ideal image of it – an enchanting promise. This form of seductive hunting resembles how advertising industry, which we discussed in Chapter 3, lures us with retouched images of a potentially achievable but still distant self-which-we-might become. We are to be seduced by a fantasy self-image as the deer is to be trapped by a false mirroring of what it might look like. The prey succumbs to the hunter only because it desires itself.[60] This desire is basically narcissistic. It is based on self-adoration, in the 'mimetic exaltation of one's own image, or rather an ideal mirage of resemblance.'[61] The future victim should be confronted by a self-image which will prove impossible to resist. The seducer's triumph depends entirely on how accurately he will resemble that image.

Perhaps inevitably, we all yearn for the ideal mirroring. Consumer society and advertising promise us the means to achieve it. We are encouraged to seek in the mirror (and document in a selfie) an image that will make us fall in love with ourselves and will make other people desire, envy, accept, 'like' or 'follow' us. It is not our present and private image that we are mostly encouraged to enjoy, but a shared, future image of us (us on vacation, us in a new car, us looking younger …) made possible by the products we ought to buy. Like the deer in the forests of the Yukaghir we might be captured by a trap baited with our own image. The mirror binds us to our self-reflection so that we think we are inseparable. It steals our love for our self and directs it to our mirroring, which has now become public. Even when we are aware of the mirror trap, we can do no more: we are condemned to look in the mirror and watch ourselves move, breathe and change as an outside spectator. So, we watch at the vision of our soulless mirrored bodies, searching for a self-image we can proudly send out into the world. We enlarge the self-image on our screens to zoom on our faces. Our gaze, the gaze of prey, full of fear, self-love and anticipation – our eyes attentive and wary. This recognition makes the gaze of the deer more familiar. It explains the face of the deer that appeared in the mirror instead of our own in Chapter 5; the peculiar, deer-like shape on the shamanic mirror in Chapter 6, the animal footprints we find on our pages. The eyes of the prey are, in this book, essentially our own. In the face of victimization, in a world which is mainly predatory, that common gaze connects humans and animals.

How to look in the mirror

Transparent illusion

Looking at oneself in the mirror is commonplace and, at the same time, 'profoundly alienating'.[1] This much is obvious from what we discussed in the previous chapters. Mirrors present us with a peculiar surface, quite different from all the other natural or artificial surfaces that surround us. The purpose of this surface is to abruptly obstruct and invert light. A mirror is nothing without light. Although any material surface reflects light, the polished mirror is made precisely for that purpose. It reflects light so well that it offers a perfect match between the observer and the observed. But as with every surface reflecting light there is a dark side as well. The illusion of transparency that the mirror offers the perceiver is the exact opposite of the opaque material reality that being close to perfectly non-absorbent of light is the distinctive feature of this object. This tension between illusion and reality is at the heart of this last chapter.

The mirror, as a reflective surface, allows to look at our body as an external delineated object. Importantly, it allows us to see parts of our body that we own and feel but otherwise cannot see. In its capacity as a visual prosthesis the mirror affords new experiential possibilities that extend our usual abilities for interoception or proprioception.[2] The basic sense of bodily self, as felt through and within the confines of the own body, is now seen and experienced outside of the body, projected onto the mirror surface. The impact of such a realization can be troubling and perceptually confusing. The exposure to one's own image in a mirror can be even traumatic,[3] especially where such exposure is fresh, as with Biami's 'terror of self-awareness' we discussed in Chapter 2, or when infants' encounter with their own specular image turns from the initial illusory social joy of meeting a playmate to an experience of wariness, fear and embarrassment, as demonstrated in the relevant psychological studies.[4] In time, familiarity with the mirror takes away any initial fear or confusion about mirror self-recognition. Yet, the perceptual anxiety of mirror gazing lingers, and, when opportunity arises, the old fears return or, worse, our mirroring creates new ones. Ageing offers an obvious example. 'In old age', as Kathleen Woodward reminds us, 'all mirrors are threatening'.[5] Old age is often construed as 'unwatchable'; the ageing body is increasingly seen as it is 'in opposition to the self' and the self is alienated from our ageing body: 'Given the western obsession with the body of youth, we can understand the "horror" of the mirror image of the decrepit body as having been produced as the inverse of the pleasures of the mirror image of the body of Narcissus.'[6]

The mirror presents us with an opportunity to appear, or in the words of Jean Baudrillard, to perform an 'appearing act'.[7] It is a visual space to which we return indefinitely in order to watch our self. Since the mirror allows us to know and negotiate the appearance of the self we have good reasons to be captured by it. In the previous chapter trying to understand what it means to be captured and seduced by our image, we escaped into the forest to observe the practice of hunting and the fate of prey. We studied the mirror as a trap capable of ensnaring most of the human and non-human persons who come into contact with it. As we've stated before, the encounter with the mirror trap lacks the finality of the poisonous arrow trap faced by an African chimpanzee. But the mirror trap is not harmless. Many times, in this book, we have described the use and abuse of the mirror to inflict, willingly or unwillingly, harm or pain on ourselves, as well as a sense of loss and despair. We have witnessed Narcissus's death caused by his own self-destructive admiration for his reflected image.

No doubt the mirror and its products (analogue or digital) have been aggressively employed by the dominant forces of market economy to promote their dream state of unfulfilled individualism based on narcissism, submissive consumerism and addiction to continuous self-tracking. As a result, it is hard to think of the mirror as having any true association with human psychosocial and emotional well-being. Still, several studies suggest otherwise. The mirror can also be a healing tool, used for caring for the self and other. It appears that the same affordances and semiotic properties that make the mirror a dangerous, potentially harmful object can be also used therapeutically. The mirror possesses healing qualities that if realized could be put to work for our benefit. Indeed, even its trickery can prove valuable. The use of mirror therapy to treat phantom limb pain in amputees is a good case in point. The term 'phantom pain' denotes in the medical literature the feeling of pain experienced by an individual concerning a part of his or her body which is no longer present. In the following section we discuss how watching the reflection of their healthy hand moving in the mirror helps the patients create a 'therapeutic illusion' of movement in the suffering/absent limb. This exercise of deliberately 'fooling themselves' in front of the mirror – that is to imagine a healthy hand moving at the side of the body where only the absence of such a hand could be witnessed – seems to have positive effect decreasing the pain. Those therapeutic dimensions of mirroring will form the focus of this final chapter.

We discuss the mirror's affordances for transparency, opacity and reflection relevant to some peculiar syndromes but also techniques of healing that could provide some unexpected insights about what happens when mirrors are looked through. Consistently with the comparative spirit of philosophical anthropology and material semiotics that characterize our approach, in this book we try to turn this illusion of transparency into a method for transforming our understanding of ordinary mirror gazing from a passive experience of self-recognition to an active medium of critical self-consciousness.

Healing

The therapeutic value of the mirror is little known and even less understood, in spite that the mirror has been used successfully[8] in many health-care settings especially in relation to eating[9] and neurologic disorders such as dementia,[10] stroke[11] and phantom pain. Various types of mirror exposure treatment (both cognitive dissonance-based and combined with mindfulness training) have proven to be an effective tool towards enhancing self-acceptance and in reducing body image disturbance in patients with eating disorders such as anorexia nervosa and bulimia nervosa.[12] However, in modern psychopathology the term 'mirror therapy' denotes primarily the analgesic function of mirror.[13] Mirror therapy has been used in a variety of pain-related syndromes, like chronic regional pain syndrome and motor-related syndromes (stroke, hand surgery) where it has improved motor control, sensory recovery and performance of activities of daily living in people with chronic stroke.[14]

The operational logic of mirror therapy is based on the dissonance created between the task performed and visual feedback[15]: Placed at specific positions (e.g. oriented parallel to the patients' midline blocking the view of the affected limb) the mirror gives the impression to the patients that what they are looking at is their impaired part of their body (let's say a hand) when in reality they are watching the reflection of their unaffected limb into the mirror. In other words, patients are 'tricked' by the mirror. A visual illusion is created whereby movement of, or touch to, the intact limb is perceived as affecting the other paretic or painful limb. This phenomenon of mirror visual feedback has the capacity to alleviate phantom limb pain or promote motor recovery after stroke.[16] In the latter case, that of hemiplegia, part of the strategy of mirror therapy involves the patients picturing their affected limb moving normally. Usually, that entails watching their healthy hand in the mirror while imagining that they are watching their impaired hand instead. Another strategy, where a therapist is involved, is assisting the patient to move the affected hand in the mirror in synchronicity with the unimpaired hand.[17] The treatments of the so-called 'phantom' pain after loss of a limb, as well as from stroke-related paralysis are probably the most famous examples where mirror visual feedback has been successfully applied in restoring brain function.

Phantom pain

The term 'phantom limb' was coined by Silas Weir Mitchell in 1872 to describe the experience, common among patients who have lost an arm or leg, of the vivid presence and severe intractable pain where the lost limb used to be. The 'phantom limb' can persist for years after amputation. The occurrence of phantom pain seems to be independent of age (although it is less frequent in young children and congenital amputees), gender and level, or side of amputation. The onset of pain, although in some cases may be delayed for months or years, is usually early with the majority of patients developing pain within the first few days after amputation. The exact aetiology of chronic phantom pain is not well understood. However, it is generally agreed that changes in the peripheral and the central nervous system following the amputation of body parts other than limbs appear to play a key role. Usually the pain is localized in distal parts of the missing limb (e.g. fingers and toes). Patients describe phantom pain as 'shooting, stabbing, boring, squeezing, throbbing, and burning' and in rare cases phantom pain may mimic pre-amputation pain in quality and in location.[18]

The basic mirror technique for treating 'phantom pain' is simple, non-invasive and widely practised. As mentioned, a portable glass mirror is vertically placed on a table and aligned with the participants' mid-sagittal plane. Participants place their intact hand in front of the mirror and their amputated limb behind the mirror. Then they perform movements of the intact limb, while looking into the mirror.[19] Or, participants have one of their hands (lost or paralysed) behind a mirror while watching the reflected image of their other unaffected hand.

Vilayanur Ramachandran and Diane Rogers-Ramachandran[20] have been pioneering in developing a mirror technique that incorporates a simple 'virtual reality box' that helps amputees to experience illusionary voluntary movement in the phantom limb in order to alleviate the pain and discomfort. That is actually a cardboard box inside of which a vertical mirror had been placed. The roof of the box had been removed and two holes are crafted on its front. The patient is told to insert both his healthy arm and his phantom arm in the box through the holes. The mirror immediately creates the illusion that the patient is now looking at two arms. In reality, the patient only observes the healthy arm and the reflection of that arm, while the absence of his amputated arm is hidden behind the mirror. The patient is then asked to move the healthy arm and observe the reflection of the arm in the mirror. This, in turn, creates the illusion that both arms obey the patient's motor commands and perform mirror symmetric movements. According to Ramachandran and Altschuler, for some patients, it is as if 'the phantom hand has been resurrected'.[21] The illusion is so powerful that people often report feeling as if their phantom, placed behind the mirror, has 'come alive'. What they actually see, objectively, is their hand's reflection inside the mirror, but what they perceive and experience subjectively is 'seeing through' the mirror's surface, as though it were actually transparent.[22] The stronger they feel and perceive the presence of their phantom behind the mirror the stronger analgesic effect it has.

There are two major explanations about why that happens. One is that the mirror exploits the brain's predilection for prioritizing visual feedback over somatosensory feedback concerning limb position. Another is that the mirror provides a visual means to 'contradict' pain: 'Ordinarily the patient feels intense pain in an arm he cannot see (his phantom). Since nothing is seen or felt other than the pain, there is nothing directly CONTRADICTING it ... '[23] (capitals in the original). Even though patients may recognize that their phantom pain cannot be real – given that their phantom limb is not real – this recognition does not seem to reduce their pain. Pain is usually immune to the powers of the intellect. Indeed, pain is reduced only when the power of 'contradiction' comes into play by technical means, namely, the use of the mirror. It is the experience of 'seeing through' the mirror's surface[24] rather than merely looking at the visual reflection of the real hand that allows the patient's brain to realize 'that there is no external object CAUSING the pain in the optically resurrected phantom' (capitals in the original), thus rejecting the pain signal as spurious.[25]

Similarly, the patient with hemiplegia who is helped by a therapist to move her impaired hand in front of the mirror might have the potential of improvement because the mirror image (of her moving a paralysed arm) contradicts her perceived inability of movement. The mirror image of her moving hand, even though assisted or just imagined, acquires, due to its effects, material substance. Not because the image is suddenly real, but because material imagination has real consequences. The image, in a way, 'happens'. The mirror, ultimately, surrenders its functionality as an object that reflects reality to become entangled with the imagination of the one who gazes in it. The mirror is no longer merely mimicking bodily movement but also disguises it by masking its weakness. Thus, on the mirror's surface, acting, perceiving, imagining and mirroring become indistinguishable from one another, turning an optical illusion into a possibility of healing.

Severed mirroring/a sickness of the gaze

Phantom pain is relevant for our broader discussion of mirror gazing also for another more general reason. Phantom pain is pain experienced at the point of absence: what is not there, not a physical part of us anymore, hurts. The general point of interest here has to do with all 'absences' that become painful in front of the mirror. We are now referring to a gaze that searches in the mirror for what is not there or what is not there any longer. It might be the case that the reflection we see in front of us lacks some characteristics that we used to have and still lingers on imagination (youth, for instance), or something we simply do not possess – a certain prototype image of what our self should look like. In both cases our gaze is met with an absence. So, while looking in the mirror is looking at our self, the self we have in mind is not necessarily the one we find in the looking-glass. Yet, the invisible characteristics are implicated in the mirror-gazing experience as we sometimes see and evaluate ourselves through them or even because of them. Youth, success, beauty or style might not be indicated in our reflection but might well be involved in our mirror gazing experience, since they are traits strenuously needed. In this sense, what is not reflected in the mirror becomes 'painful' in the way an absent limb does. It is ultimately the pain of that which does not exist, the pain of absence. The body suffers a mock separation; the actual mirror image appears somehow distorted and incomplete. Coming back to our discussion of the mirror trap in the previous chapter, this mock separation is one of the major ways the mirror hurts its victims: instead of poisonous arrows or iron claws, it inflicts on its human prey the pain of the ideal mirroring. This ideal mirroring is always absent, thus the 'phantom-wound'.

It is not our reflection – what is actually there in the mirror – that produces the pain and dissatisfaction. Rather, it is the 'rival reflection', the invisible self we crave for that causes bewilderment and self-doubt. Even though we can step in and out of the mirror trap as many times as we like, that invisible self will never appear in our reflection – it only acts as bait to draw us into the mirror trap. The 'rival reflection' disturbs self-awareness and self-appreciation; it is a most insistent reminder of what the mirror spectator is deficient in. The 'rival reflection' takes shape in our imagination: for instance, through the image of the happy consumer on which capitalistic society depends to feed itself. It acts as an imaginary body that is caught up between the lived body and the body reflected in the mirror. In the end, the idea we have of ourselves is not built through experience and experimentation, but through disorientation and narcissism.

The mirrored body seldom lives up to expectations. There is always something missing between the seeing and the seen. The 'phantom-wound' remains open. At a deeper level, mirror gazing becomes an experience of missing self-parts: we become, in our minds, amputees. The severed gaze focuses on what the reflected body does not possess; it 'maims' our mirrored self. The one looking feels amputated despite of the body in the mirror appearing whole. It is a sickness of the gaze.

Social mirrors

This absent or phantom body, like anything else bodily, is both imaginary and real. On the one hand, the phantom body is imaginary because, at the conscious reflective level, it is partly a story narrated (or more accurately a collection of stories inscribed in the course of our life history) and partly a memory re-enacted. On the other hand, the phantom body is real because unlike other stories narrated (e.g. by means of language), bodily stories must be performed or else they don't carry conviction or have meaning. Bodily inscription is incorporation. Of course, the stories we tell of ourselves in front of the mirror can only ever be partial. They are stories of unknown origin and unclear ending. This kind of anticipatory personal narrative becomes easily absorbed into, or dominated by, available socio-political discourses of subjectivation. It is those discourses that often determine our self-narratives about what the body is and does, about how it should look or behave. The mentioned phantom body is a hybrid creature composed of this creative synergy or tension between our bodily selfhood and our narrative selfhood.[26]

Many times, in this book we wrote about pre-conceived ideas of the self-image, in the form of stereotypes, practices and norms imposed on us by consumerist society and market economy. Before gazing in the mirror, before even standing in front of it, we have in our minds a set of predictions and anticipations on how our self-image will be judged, evaluated, accepted or rejected; how it will fare in relation to the images of other people.

Mirror gazing, like any other skill, is subject to normative assessment and social scrutiny. First of all, by looking in the mirror we become immediately aware of how we look in relation with other people. What we see in the mirror is also what other people see when they look at us. The appearance of the specular image inherits (for better or worse) the concerns of one's community. As social creatures we want our mirroring to conform to our expectations of how we should look like in the eyes of others.

The ontogenetic origins of this basic relationship between mirror gazing and our need to 'fit in' has been demonstrated also experimentally.[27] In particular, young children's (fourteen to fifty-two months) response to the mirror mark test was explored in different social contexts to see whether normative factors 'such as the need to match the appearance of self to the appearance of others' may influence children's mirror self-recognition behaviour.[28] The experimental procedure entailed two major conditions: in the first condition yellow 'post-it' stickers where placed only on the forehead of children. Most children passed the test, demonstrating a tendency to touch and remove the mark off of their forehead. In the second condition, everyone in the room, the child, experimenter and accompanying parent, were marked prior to the child's mirror exposure with similar 'post-it' stickers on their forehead. Children were now less likely to touch or remove their mark 'often putting it back on their forehead in an apparent attempt at conforming with the social norm established in the testing room'.[29] What these findings suggest is that 'children passing the mark test do not construe the mirror reflection solely in terms of its reference to the embodied self, but are also capable of construing such reflection in reference to how others might perceive and evaluate them'.[30] Cognition, Philippe Rochat and Dan Zahavi write, is not the only thing involved in the mirror experience 'but also a sensitivity and awareness of evaluative others as well as a conformity to perceived social norms, what is allowed or promoted by the culture, and what is not'.[31] The manifestation of mirror self-recognition, at least in humans, always involves others. A labour on self-presentation, self-correction of public appearance, all signs of 'normative conformity'[32] are the trademarks of the mirror self-experience.

The main trait of the mirror is to make us aware of ourselves by making our bodies visible. In fact, the mirror is unique at not letting us escape ourselves. While any other object around us gives us such opportunity, providing us with the visual distraction of all that is not us, the mirror traps our gaze in our reflection and throws 'ourselves' back on us. Our gaze is now world-blind. The body sees itself seeing, examines itself examining. Vision, in front of a mirror, is not liberty from the self; it is chained to an image that is 'outside' as a portrait might be, but is not independent of us, unaware of us, there without us.

Our mirror double – to which, if we raise our right hand in salute it will raise its left – exercises on us a kind of thought and emotional control. By turning our body into a spectacle the mirror makes us more willing to conform to the social norm of public appearance. The mirror makes us more compliant. We might say that the mirror image is forcing us to behave in ways that are not always meaningful for us but that, nonetheless, make good sense when we think with *others in mind*[33] – like walking about carrying a yellow 'post-it' sticker stuck on our foreheads because everyone else around us does so.

Is there any space for resistance?

Body without organs

Gilles Deleuze and Félix Guattari's notion of the 'Body Without Organs' is relevant here. The French playwright Antonin Artaud was the first to introduce this notion as a means to be done with God's judgement. For Artaud there can't be any such judgement unless there are organs. Our organs allow for us to be judged and controlled. Therefore, a body without organs is a body liberated. It is also a body freed from social, biological and political censorship: a body open to experimentation, and, if we exercise caution, a body free of repression. Organs: static, fixed, bind to the skin; organized and organizing, unable of change. Deleuze and Guattari urge us to find a way to make a body without organs for ourselves. 'It's a question of life and death, youth and old age, sadness and joy. It is where everything is played out.'[34] A body without organs is experimentation. At the same time, it is a limit and a process of becoming. A body without organs is a set of practices. To have one in your life is inevitable:

> On it we sleep, live our waking lives, fight – fight and are fought – seek our place, experience untold happiness and fabulous defeats; on it we penetrate and are penetrated; on it we love ... Your body without organs is already

there, waiting for you. But you can fail; mess it up. You may end up with a body which is dry, stupefied, a body without gaiety, ecstasy and dance.[35]

How can the habit of mirror gazing be fruitfully brought in to this process? To begin with, mirror gazing provides us with a vision our bodies: skin, eyes, ears, nose, mouth, etc. None of those organs, nevertheless, are truly there on the glass. What we actually view is an empty reflection, a vision of an organ-less self. Truly, the double in the mirror is lacking in everything: a drained shell instead of Deleuze and Guattari's full egg; a flat, virtual body instead of a full, living one. It is interesting (for us), it intrigues us, only because we desperately want to learn things about ourselves. Our mirroring, obviously, possesses no organs; it has no substance, no bodily limitation. Does it set us free? Unfortunately, no. Not automatically. As we discussed, what we initially experience when we first look into the mirror is a sense of displacement, a bilocation. Our self relocates and becomes a reflection. We exchange a real self with a mirror image. In fact, it is more of a distraction than an exchange. The mirror image resembles a body that loses everything at once by a too-sudden dislocation – a phantom that stands on the ruins of our physical selves. Perhaps, then, we have provided a possible answer to Edmund Carpenter's question about the tribal terror of self-awareness (see Chapter 2). There is something frightening to a self that all of a sudden relocates, deprived of everything: flesh, organs, warmth, heartbeat, breath. The knowledge of our body is disturbed by the presence of our organ-less mirror double and our sense of personal identity weakens. The terror of bilocation is not only one of sudden self-awareness, as Carpenter assumes, but also one of transformation – an abrupt becoming-an-image that accompanies the first glimpses of self-recognition.

This becoming-an-image is essential for society's control over us. Easier than controlling a body is to control an image that body aspires to. The mirror image is binding. It binds us with society: with the social eye. Because what we see in the mirror is what another person sees when looking at us, the social eye becomes, in a way, our own. A new awareness. An adopted eye making us aware of our appearance to the world. So, despite its lack of organs, the mirrored body has other ways to organize and regulate our behaviour. Artaud's desire to be done with judgement through an organ-less body, we mentioned before, seems to be working in reverse: the more we look in the mirror the more we become aware of our self as a social spectacle.

On seeing through

The mirror takes us 'out there'; it exposes our visibility to others. In the mirror, Merleau-Ponty wrote, 'my externality becomes complete'.[36] All that is secret passes into the face reflection, that 'flat, closed being' of which we were only dimly aware from seeing our reflections in the water. How should we deal with this exposure? For Merleau-Ponty, the face in the mirror is an opportunity for self-knowledge and transgressive embodiment. A face is what we see and at the same time something we must learn how to look at. Common experience and phenomenology tell us that the body, whose face we are looking at, is more than a bundle of well-assembled tissues, surfaces and organs. We have every good reason to assume that there is a self, our self, which is inseparably linked with that body we see in the mirror. But 'how do I know the person I see in the mirror is really me?'[37] Why assume that it is our body, rather than a stranger, that we see in the mirror? We assume it is our body because it looks like we do, moves when we move and we see it being touched when we touch ourselves. That basic sensation can be challenged, leading to various forms of mirrored-self misidentification associated with the delusional belief that one's reflection in the mirror is a stranger. Indeed, as a 'hard-won' but also 'slightly unstable' evolutionary and developmental accomplishment, mirror self-recognition has proven most vulnerable, especially in the context of neurodegenerative disease.[38] Take for instance mirror agnosia, a condition where the person seems to believe that the mirrored image is real (not a reflection) and the real object is inside the mirror or behind the mirror. When people with this condition are asked to localize and grasp the object reflected in the mirror instead of looking for the original object in its real place, they try repeatedly to grasp the objects inside the mirror. Paradoxically such persons are clearly able to recognize the mirror as an object. They know what mirror is and does; they identify the frame and the glass of the mirror and know that they look at it. Yet, they seem unable to use that knowledge when interacting with mirrors as if they are locked inside the looking-glass. The so-called 'mirror sign' is another characteristic form of mirror agnosia. Patients are now able to identify the real locations of the reflected objects as coming from behind as well as to recognize other people's reflections in the mirror and to define the reflective properties of mirrors, but are unable or have great difficulty to 'recognize one's own mirrored reflection'.[39] Instead of seeing one's reflection in the mirror, what they see is a stranger that could be a friend, an enemy or a god.[40] Not only they entertain the delusional belief that the person they see in the mirror is not themselves, they also seem to maintain this belief when challenged.[41]

What can we learn? We believe that those occasions of impediment and mental disruption, strange and profoundly troubling as they may be, or they may seem to be, for the patients involved, offer us the equivalent of a borderless mirror, that is a mirror that invites and allows exactly the kind of 'abnormal' exchange or participation that 'normal' people are usually denied in their daily encounters with the looking-glass. We should be looking closer at those 'abnormal' participatory exchanges and try to benefit from the insights that they offer.

Looking into the mirror is easy but finding oneself in the mirror requires skill: you must both learn and unlearn how to see. Without that skill the mirror will merely trap our gaze like prey. It will reflect without revealing. Our ways of seeing are not given or fixed. Seeing is an act of creation more than it is a re-presentation. As such, meaning and self-awareness are not guaranteed on the mirror's surface. In spite of the repetitive character of our everyday ritual of mirror gazing, coming to terms with our ever-changing image is not always successful. We need to embrace this uncertainty. To remember is also to forget. Perhaps sometimes the healthy thing to do is to gaze at our mirrored face (or at least pretend) from a state of amnesia, as if we know or remember nothing about it. In those rare occasions we allow ourselves to being transformed; we let the mirror do its magic. When that happens our phantom-self becomes alive. The mirror has to succumb to the change as well: it has to 'hide' itself. In order for our gaze to become flexible and adventurous the mirror should give up something of its rigidity. To see through an object, the object must somehow cease to be an object, that is, it must lose its objecthood and turn into a thing. Things are diluted entities, open and undefined. In that sense mirroring becomes *thinging*[42]: an act of thinking and feeling with and through the mirror. The mirror opens up its borders.

In different chapters of this book we talked of such an unorthodox experience. In literature, the mirror compromises its materiality, its glass, for Carroll's Alice to step through or Borges' mirror people to enter our realm. In Plath's poetry, the mirror fills up with water for a terrible fish to swim in it. In the case of the shamanic mirror in Mongolia we tried to unlearn our assumptions and to look 'through' the mirror as if it was transparent. In the forests of the Yukaghir, the body of the hunter itself becomes a mirror to sexually seduce his prey. To end this book, we return to this primary experience of 'seeing through' to explore its healing properties. One deeply entrenched assumption about the mirror is that the mirror image cannot lie. Remember the words of Umberto Eco from Chapter 2: one 'cannot lie with and through a mirror image'.[43] Still, it is sometimes necessary, as in the case of the healing mirror box we discussed above, to purposefully fall for appearances. In the phantom limb experiments the visual message of a healthy, obedient hand in the mirror evades the reality of its absence. The mirror becomes, in the patient's mind, transparent: the intended reflection eliminates the object. Tricking the body into looking through the mirror at something which is not actually there seems to bypass the pain. Looking in the mirror the patient or amputee confuses the image of the hand reflected on the mirror's surface for the lost or paralysed hand that is actually hidden behind the mirror. Gazing through the looking-glass, therefore, sometimes produces a 'fiction' that heals.

The mirror, however, rarely becomes transparent on its own. Seeing through or beyond the mirror is, in the case of mirror therapy, the result of deliberate and organized effort. Falling for appearances is often needed in order to gain new access to the reality of our existence. That reality is very hard to see with our naked eyes: our imagination should also be recruited. Imagination, here, does not denote the kind of 'mental imaging' that happens when the world is not present or when the body is sleeping. Imagination here is enactive; it denotes the kind of material imagination[44] that helps us see with and through the mirror. However, mirror looking, as it is practised in our modern culture, is deprived of material imagination. A mirror window through which mirror images could come in or go out is something we would allow only in fiction. Therefore, to us, the mirror surface remains impermeable. And so, one way or another, the mirror fails us. It fails because no bridge is established between mirroring and imagining. More accurately though, it is our gaze that fails. This lack of imaginative engagement, through and with the mirror, often renders it an uneventful and oppressive device. Yet, by no means is this the only way, or the natural way, to look at the mirror.

As young children with innocent eyes we used to look 'through' the mirror. Probably it took us only a couple of days to learn that there is nothing to reach and grab for other than a solid reflective surface. We learned to take a different perceptual stance towards the mirror: to look 'at' the mirror rather than 'through' it. Unlearning that perceptual habit is not as easy. The experience of transparency is lost in the adult modern world. We no longer remember how to look through the mirror. We cannot even imagine what it feels like to do so. In those rare occasions that the experience of transparency returns, it is no longer the sign of playfulness, enactive discovery and re-enchantment, but of mental impairment as with the case of mirror agnosia we discussed. Does this have to be the case?

Metamorphoses: The gaze of the hunter

We believe that retaining or re-discovering the ability to look through the mirror is possible and can be also therapeutic. We are gesturing towards a new kind of mirror exposure, one that promotes a therapeutic alliance between self and the mirror. This alliance is comparable to the alliance between the hunter and the prey we explored in the previous chapter. Looking through the mirror demands that in our engagement with the mirror we abandon the gaze of prey and adopt the gaze of the hunter. What does this mean?

Prey usually sees whatever the hunter intends. The hunter knows the needs of the prey and so is able to manipulate its behaviour and movements. In our own visual culture that seems to feed on self-images; our steps are directed in front of a mirror – real or imaginary, traditional or digital. Standing there, our self-love grows, so does our need. As far as self-direction is concerned, shedding the skin of the prey and becoming a hunter means to stop being herded around. It also means we have to strike a balance: living life in front of the mirror is to exhaust the relationship with oneself. That is to adopt the gaze of prey or in some cases that of a predator. A hunter's gaze, instead, would never be self-consuming.

The philosopher Michael Foucault remarked in an interview in 1984 that an important duty of philosophy is its critical function: 'the challenging of all phenomena of domination at whatever level or under whatever form they present themselves-political, economic, sexual, institutional, and so on. This critical function of philosophy, up to a certain point, emerges right from the Socratic imperative: "Be concerned with yourself, i.e., ground yourself in liberty, through the mastery of self."[45] So, what we are after here can be described as critical mirroring, that is, mirroring for critical self-consciousness. This is the consciousness that one develops only by adopting the gaze of the hunter. The procedure has many risks and demands caution. Like the Yukaghir hunter we run the risk of losing ourselves – of becoming that elusive other that lives inside the mirror. Still how we look in the mirror should be our choice.

This remaking of gaze is part of a broader strategy for transforming our ecology of perception: our ways of seeing and of thinking inside the world. That move presupposes a great deal of unlearning. But a hunter is nothing if not flexible and inventive. The gaze of the hunter refers to an ability to see the world differently. In our case that means seeing the self-reflection differently: a hunter would choose when and how to gaze in the mirror and what to 'read' in it. The opposite is a habitual and often mechanical way of looking: the lethargic and self-absorbed gaze of a victim repeatedly falling into the mirror trap, learning nothing. The gaze of the hunter is an invitation to see the mirror's enchantment and not just its glass: to find oneself in the mirror but also in the mirror's depths. Acquiring such a gaze means that we do not exhaust our relationship with our image. The gaze of the hunter is open to possibilities, subject to constant change and re-evaluation. Crucially, the gaze of the hunter touches on the mirror lightly. The effected transformation is worth the effort. The mirror opens up to new possibilities of participatory sense-making and endless opportunities of looking at, with, through and in. A new ecology of mirroring thus emerges, one in which our most deeply entrenched recollections, projections and anticipations can be challenged and exchanged. Mimesis is now transformed into critical self-consciousness.

Epilogue

The relation with the mirror that we have set out to describe in this book cannot be perceived from a single perspective point. People, in different situations, times and places, do not necessarily perceive the same thing when they look in the mirror – their senses and bodies can be differentially attuned to it. They look in it differently. In the previous chapters we have sought to reveal the varieties of mirror gazing and to understand their agency and impact in human life and selfhood. We were thus concerned with the use and abuse of the mirror, and especially of the mirroring, as a cross-cultural medium of self-identification. To this end, the book directed to the mirror an explorative anthropological gaze intended at enactive discovery.[1] The goal has been to turn the mirror into a creative apparatus of experimentation and of self-transformation.

By way of conclusion we return to the crucial question we raised at the start of the previous chapter: What does it mean and what does it take to recognize oneself in a mirror? Finding oneself in the mirror is not as easy as we may think. Often it is not our hand that holds the mirror; it is not our face or body that we see reflected in it. Whose body or face is that? Whose hand is holding the mirror? In this book we tried to show that self and the other, individual and society, hold the mirror together. Sometimes in harmony, resembling the participatory exchanges of the Amazonian Tukanos, sometimes pulling it in opposite directions, resembling the asymmetrical predatory spirit of the Jivaro tribes. The body is in the middle: never just an 'I' or a social 'me'. The self is where the bodily 'I' and the social 'me' meet. The mirror can facilitate but also disrupt this meeting.

The practice of mirror gazing establishes an open circuit between the body that sees the seeing body undergoing constant transformation (biological, cognitive, social and technical). The bodily self that is visible in the mirror may well be disturbed (e.g. by ageing, by accident, by disease) and obstructed. Our self-image can be extended and mediated; it can also become burdened by parts that do not belong to it. In that sense, the mirror trap might even be considered like a training terrain for the practice of 'being seen', of realizing the self as image.

According to the mirror self-recognition test, a child's touching of a mark on the body, once discovered in the mirror, is interpreted as an explicit index of self-awareness. When a Western Samoan child, studied by Philippe Rochat, confronted with his mirror reflection after a yellow Post-It sticker was surreptitiously placed on the top of his forehead, he immediately identifies it, and reaches for it to touch it or to remove it.[2] Throughout the course of our lives, we are surreptitiously marked. Usually we do not bother to understand the nature of those marks. We take self-awareness for granted. We have stopped wondering what we see when we see ourselves in a mirror. Self-recognition is now diminishing to mere object recognition. At best, we behave like a face recognition software. If the marks are internal, inscribed beneath the skin, often we do not even realize that we have been marked. But even when we do see the marks we seem uncertain about what exactly we should do with them. Those marks are different. Unlike the innocent rouge or stickers in use when children and animals are tested in the mirror mark, these marks cannot be easily removed once we perceive them. They remain unbeknownst and attached to our skin. They become our second skin; what Terence Turner would call 'social skin'.[3]

We have spoken about memory in scars before, saying that the lines and marks of our face are threads and traces of personal narrative (see Chapter 3). They mark and preserve our history. We also pointed out that extreme cosmetic techniques used for beautification, such as plastic surgery, can be seen as an implicit attempt to do the opposite – a sort of depersonalization: amnesia forced on the skin that, in certain aspects, equalizes the phenomenal amnesia induced to the body during the *tsantsa* preparation of the Jivaro tribes. Here, we took the opportunity to underline a way in which personal identity is seen to be communicated not through facial features but more through the 'history of a face'.

To explain, the modern industries of beautification promote a false narrative about the mirror self-image in which personal identity is often presented as something intimately associated with specific aesthetic or facial qualities as they manifest on the human skin. The implicit message, damage on the skin is damage on the self, perhaps explains why the increased concern to repair ageing skin or face is not a mere aesthetic issue but also a deeper attempt to reclaim or restore personal identity which is perceived as being threatened by time. Still, the beautiful and timeless face at the centre of this narrative of beautification is an illusion. It is not a real face. It is a face deprived of memory and thus of humanity. It is a face already disconnected from the person whose pathway in life and emotional state was meaning to signify. It may be a beautiful face. But it is also a face that can be commercialized – a saleable face. A face from which the traces of time and life history have been erased is a face without critical consciousness.

Succumbing to this narrative about the mirror self-image, we are deceived by our own reflection and become the prey of our own trap. One of Damien Hirst's early art installations from 1990, *A Thousand Years*, offers an extremely powerful and unexpected means to visualize that. Hirst presented a glass box with the decaying head of a cow trapped inside it. The head bred maggots that turned to flies. Inside the glass box, there was also a trap for flies – the sort of a trap which attracts flies on its high voltage light and burns them. 'A trap within a trap', Alfred Gell wrote about that installation: 'Victims within a victim.'[4] With critical mirroring the face can no longer be discredited by age, damage, change, difference or appearance. Moreover, the marking of that face through time, experience and personal narrative becomes the primary source of its affective power and aesthetic appeal. Such a face or body is now viewed as part of a common humanity, a shared destiny, a testimony to communal existence and awareness of death.

The challenge we face in front of the mirror can also be expressed in the form of a Foucauldian imperative with two related components: The first is how to take proper 'care' of our bodies. The second is how to reclaim our critical self-consciousness. To answer these challenges, one needs to re-learn how to look in the mirror: what to expect, what to appreciate, what to disregard completely, what to remember and what to forget. This is not an easy task. Under the spell of modernism and the capitalist ethos of consumerism, mirror gazing increasingly becomes an endangered skill. Capitalist society realized that in order to control consumption habits it needs to control desire. As Bernard Stiegler notes, capitalism is concerned not only with increased productivity but also with winning the libido of the consumers.[5] The image industry constantly tries to capture our attention and feed our imagination with uniform images of how we should look like. The image maker tries, in other words, to manipulate people's desire and consciousness regarding how they should appear, and, as a consequence, their mirror gaze. Market economy needs a consumer 'whose behaviour is standardised through the formation and artificial manufacturing of his desires'.[6] By depriving people of their individuality, 'hyper-industrial' society produces 'herds of beings lacking being – and lacking becoming, that is, lacking a future'.[7] This leads us to note that the word 'desire', in this book, has a specific meaning. In the idiom of Deleuze and Guattari, desire denotes a feeling characterized by productive energy and the absence of lack. A desire lacking in nothing, independent of pleasure and infused with joy: 'a joy that is immanent to desire as though desire were filled by itself and its contemplations, a joy that implies no lack or impossibility and is not measured by pleasure since it is what distributes intensities of pleasure and prevents them from being suffused by anxiety, shame, and guilt.'[8] To desire in such a way, when looking in the mirror, is to experience a sort of completeness. A lack of lacking. This, nevertheless, means to be able to accept our self-image for what it is: individual and unique. This is the kind of desire we are after. This is also the kind of desire the mirror image is most resistant to.

Yet, the truth of the matter is that in front of the mirror all humans are equals. In facilitating us to view ourselves from the 'outside', the mirror enables us to compare our image with that of other people. It allows, consequently, for a sort of antagonism to arise – sometimes a fierce one. Still, we must acknowledge: in the mirror-gazing 'competition' everybody is given the same chance. Rich or poor, you glance in the same mirror to face what everybody else is facing. The logic of capitalism has no real power; it is the art of looking that matters. The mirroring cannot be bought or exchanged. Unlike any other prestige commodity or medium of self-presentation, its value is not negotiable. Supposing that a mirror's glass is not cracked or otherwise damaged, the standard household looking-glass will produce the same service whether framed on gold or on plain metal, rusted around the edges. And it does so regardless of the person that stands in front of it: a king and a beggar would have the same treatment. Mirroring is freely available. It resists equally the desire of all people, powerful or underprivileged. Thus, the mirror is, we declare, one of the rare objects of democracy. An equalizer. The mirror can't be bribed. In order to change our mirroring, we have to change ourselves: the way we look in the mirror.

To accomplish this transformation, we can only count on ourselves. The mirror image will not transform to meet our desire or to accommodate our self-narratives (not even our psychopathologies). Even when 'we' move in the mirror, the mirror remains still; its basic function and its physical properties are not changing. We can come closer or move further away from the mirror's surface, but the mirror itself provides a fixed and unambiguous point of reference. There is a notable tension here that is important to point out: since early prehistory, images co-evolve with human perception. Different kinds of images and ways of imaging will bring about different kinds of perception and ways of seeing.[9] The image, like most things that matter in human life, is not a fixed thing but a dynamic process. As Hans Belting observes, 'every image, once it has fulfilled its current mission, generates a new image'.[10] That much seems inevitable – the photographic or the cinematic image, for instance, has withstood drastic transformation since their invention. Yet, Belting's just remark cannot apply to the mirroring. For all the decades to come, and for all that has been, the mirroring remains the same. There is something, however, that we must make a note of, a new phenomenon: the mirror selfie. Through the mirror selfie, the mirroring 'escaped' the confines of its own material medium and entered the world of digital photography and media culture. In a sense, the mirror image invaded photography acquiring, thus, two features it never had: permanence and sociability. The mirroring may now be 'arrested' in a picture and sent travelling into the world of social media: it has an audience. We consider the mirror selfie as a hybrid technology brought about by the synergy of the mirroring and the photographic camera: a new image that has deeply and irrevocably affected our desire, behaviour and the way we gaze at and present ourselves to the world. At this point, nevertheless, we are writing about the mirroring. And the mirroring alone, without the digital gaze of a smartphone, has not changed. It is what it is. Here then lies the tension of paradox: there is only one type of mirroring. In a most restricting way, the mirror has a single visual story to tell. But our gaze does not. Our gaze is a force that never rests. 'Our vision', John Berger remarks, 'is continually active, continually moving, continually holding things in a circle around itself'.[11] In our book, we tried to point out that the mirroring might be set, chained to its place and material, but our vision is, most emphatically, our own. Personal instead of public. Moving instead of static. The mirror creates and maintains an illusion of pictorial objectivity of absolute truths. But we all look at things differently: there is no such thing as a universal gaze. What we see in the mirror is already partly constructed, mediated and transformed. We never simply look at our mirroring. To look in the mirror is to build a bridge: our gaze establishes a connection between our felt body and our mirror image through which we come to know and recognize ourselves. We say that the way we look in the mirror is reflected in the narratives we make about ourselves. The mirroring, in this sense, is a strikingly powerful image and, in our times, perhaps the most important.

To end, we return to where we started: a deer gazing in a mirror we set up in an imaginary clearing of a forest. Through the course of our book we realized that the mirror was a trap. We saw the deer falling in it as something both expected and inevitable. We, therefore, started to think of mirror gazing as a story about hunting and we came upon a clue, an insight: we, like the deer, are prey in front of the mirror. An unusual kind of prey, for we are also the ones making and setting up mirrors. There is a definite sense of agency and control about our relationship with mirrors. And yet, as we examined this relationship closer, we had to admit that the way we are directed in front of mirrors (sometimes with a smartphone in hand) confirms the idea that it is very possible for humans to become prey to their own self-reflection. So, let's imagine we now go and stand next to the deer. Our gazes meet in the looking-glass. We propose an alliance – a gaze that connects. This way of looking will allow us to reclaim ownership of our body (physical and virtual). Do we still pass the test of mirror self-recognition? We certainly do. Passing the test is easy. But perhaps the true challenge with our daily test of mirror self-recognition is elsewhere: perhaps we should try failing it.

Notes

Chapter 1

1   Philippe Rochat and Zahavi Dan, 'The uncanny mirror: A re-framing of mirror self-experience', *Consciousness and Cognition* 20:2 (2011), pp. 204–13.

    For a concise history of the human fascination with the mirror, see Mark Pendergrast, *Mirror Mirror: A History of the Human Love Affair with Reflection* (New York: Basic Books, 2003). For a recent collection of essays on this topic, see Miranda Anderson, ed., *The Book of the Mirror: An Interdisciplinary Collection Exploring the Cultural History of the Mirror* (Newcastle: Cambridge Scholars Publishing, 2007).

2   The word 'mirroring' can be understood both as a noun and a verb; we will use it to designate both the process of mirror gazing and its product.

3   Philippe Rochat, 'Origin of self-concept', in G. Bremner and A. Foge, eds., *Blackwell Handbook of Infant Development* (Oxford: Blackwell, 2001), pp. 191–212.

4   See Chapter 2.

5   Rochat and Zahavi, 'The uncanny mirror'.

6   Gibson, J. J., The ecological approach to visual perception, Hillsdale, NJ: Lawrence Erlbaum Associates, 1979.

7   Roland Barthes, *Camera Lucida* (London: Vintage, 1993), p. 13.

8   Umberto Eco, *Semiotics and the Philosophy of Language* (Bloomington: Indiana University Press, 1984), p. 207.

9   This was first observed by art historian Ernst H. Gombrich in his classic, *Art and Illusion* (Oxford: Phaidon Press, 1960), p. 5.

10 See the discussion of relevant phenomena and psychiatric studies in Chapters 2 and 3.

11 For a good review of some experimental evidence on people's beliefs about how the size of mirror images changes with distance, see Marco Bertamini and Theodore E. Parks, 'On what people know about images on mirrors', *Cognition* 98:1 (2005), pp. 85–104.

12 Lambros Malafouris, *How Things Shape the Mind: A Theory of Material Engagement* (Cambridge, MA: MIT Press, 2013).

13 Tim Ingold and Gisli Palsson, eds., *Biosocial Becomings: Integrating Social and Biological Anthropology* (Cambridge: Cambridge University Press, 2013).

14 Jane Bennett, *Vibrant Matter: A Political Ecology of Things* (Durham, NC: Duke University Press, 2010). Diane Coole and Samantha Frost, 'Introducing the new materialisms', in Pheng Cheah, Melissa A. Orlie, and Elizabeth Grosz, eds., *New Materialisms: Ontology, Agency, and Politics* (Durham, NC: Duke University Press, 2010), pp. 1–43.

15 Martin Holbraad and Morten Axel Pedersen, *The Ontological Turn: An Anthropological Exposition* (Cambridge: Cambridge University Press, 2016).

16 In Barad's performative sense, see Karen Barad, 'Posthumanist performativity: Toward an understanding of how matter comes to matter', *Signs: Journal of Women in Culture and Society* 28:3 (2003), pp. 801–31. Karen Barad, *Meeting the Universe Halfway: Quantum Physics and the Entanglement of Matter and Meaning* (Durham, NC: Duke University Press, 2007).

17 In the context of Jane Bennett's theory of 'vibrant matter', the term 'vitality' refers to 'the capacity of things – edibles, commodities, storms, metals – not only to impede or block the will and designs of humans but also to act as quasi agents or forces with trajectories, propensities, or tendencies of their own'. Bennett's main aspiration with this theory 'is to articulate a vibrant materiality that runs alongside and inside humans to see how analyses of political events might change if we gave the force of things more due' (Bennett, *Vibrant Matter*, p. viii). This conception of vitality is of course very close in meaning, and partly it derives from the terms 'actant' or 'actantiality', which occupy a prominent place in the vocabulary of Actor-Network Theory (ANT) as developed among others by the prominent anthropologist of modernity Bruno Latour. See Bruno Latour *Reassembling the Social: An Introduction to Actor-Network-Theory* (Oxford: Oxford University Press, 2007). Malafouris have developed a related material engagement approach proposing notions of metaplasticity and material agency; see Malafouris, *How Things Shape the Mind*.

18 Gregory Bateson, *Mind and Nature. A Necessary Unity* (New York: Bentam Books, 1979), p. 14.

19 Tim Ingold, *The Life of Lines* (Abingdon-on-Thames: Routledge, 2015).

20 Ibid.

21 Gilles Deleuze and Félix Guattari, *Rhizôme, Introduction* (Paris: Editions de Minuit, 1976). Gilles Deleuze and Félix Guattari, *A Thousand Plateaus: Capitalism and Schizophrenia* (London: Bloomsbury Publishing, 1988).

22 Tim Ingold, *Being Alive: Essays on Movement, Knowledge and Description* (Abingdon-on-Thames: Taylor & Francis, 2011), p. 160, emphasis in original.

23 Malafouris, L., 'Thinking as "thinging": Psychology with things', Current Directions in Psychological Science 29:1 (2020), pp. 3–8.

24 Caroline Humphrey, 'Inside and outside the mirror: Mongolian Shamans' mirrors as instruments of perspectivism', *Inner Asia* 9 (2007), pp. 173–95.

25 Alfred Gell, 'Vogel's net: Traps as artworks and artworks as traps', *Journal of Material Culture* 1:1 (1996), pp. 15–38.

26 Rane Willerslev, 'Not animal, not not-animal: Hunting, imitation, and empathetic knowledge among the Siberian Yukaghirs', *Journal of the Royal Anthropological Institute* 10 (2004), pp. 629–52; Rane Willerslev, *Soul Hunters: Hunting, Animism, and Personhood among the Siberian Yukaghirs* (London: University of California Press, 2007).

Chapter 2

1 Hans Belting, *An Anthropology of Images: Picture, Medium, Body* (Princeton NJ: Princeton University Press, 2011), pp. 9–10.

2 Lambros Malafouris and Colin Renfrew, eds., *The Cognitive Life of Things: Recasting the Boundaries of the Mind* (Cambridge, UK: McDonald Institute for Archaeological Research, 2010).

3 Eco, *Semiotics and the Philosophy of Language*, p. 211.

4 Gordon G. Gallup, James R. Anderson, and Steven M. Platek, 'Self-recognition', in Shaun Gallagher, ed., *The Oxford Handbook of the Self* (Oxford: Oxford University Press, 2011), pp. 1–55, 15–16.

5 Eco, *Semiotics and the Philosophy of Language*, p. 210.

6 William J.T. Mitchell, 'What is an image?' *New Literary History* 15 (1984), pp. 503–37, 503.

7 Foucault, M., The care of the self: The history of sexuality, Volume 3, New York: Pantheon, 1986.

8 Eco, *Semiotics and the Philosophy of Language*, p. 207.

9 Bertamini and Parks, 'On what people know about images on mirrors', pp. 85–104.

10 Rochat and Zahavi, 'The uncanny mirror', p. 2.

11 Ibid.

12 https://www.youtube.com/watch?v=0nmu3uwqzbI (see 0:55). *Ghost Dance* is an independent, improvisation British film relished in 1983. It explores the concept of 'Ghosts', memory and technology, especially cinema. It is directed by Ken McMullen. Screenplay by Ken McMullen.

13 Ibid., 1:05.

14 Lambros Malafouris, 'Learning to see: Enactive discovery and the prehistory of pictorial skill', in Klaus Sachs-Hombach and Jörg R.J. Schirra, eds., *Origins of Pictures: Anthropological Discourses in Picture Science* (Köln: Halem Verlag, 2012), pp. 73–88.

15 The term 'bilocation' describes instances in which an individual is or appears to feel located in two distinct places at the same time. For a good review of the literature relevant to the issue of self-localization, see Bartholomäus Wissmath, David Weibel, Jan Schmutz, and Fred W. Mast, 'Being present in more than one place at a time? Patterns of mental self-localization', *Consciousness and Cognition*, 20:4 (2011), pp. 1808–15.

16 Malafouris, *Learning to See*.

17 O. J. Grüsser and T. Landis, 'The splitting of "I" and "me": Heautoscopy and related phenomena', *Visual Agnosias and Other Disturbances of Visual Perception and Cognition* 12 (1991), pp. 297–303. Blanke Olaf and Shahar Arzy, 'The out-of-body experience: Disturbed self-processing at the temporo-parietal junction', *The Neuroscientist* 11:1 (2005), pp. 16–24.

18 Barthes, *Camera Lucida*.

19 Ibid., p. 13.

20 Francesca Anzellotti, Valeria Onofrj, Valerio Maruotti, Leopoldo Ricciardi, Raffaella Franciotti, Laura Bonanni, Astrid Thomas, and Marco Onofrj, 'Autoscopic phenomena: Case report and review of literature', *Behavioral and Brain Functions* 7:2 (2011), p. 2.

21 Ibid., p. 3.

22 The German word 'Doppelganger' was introduced in 1796 by the novelist Jean Paul Richter, who defined the word as follows: 'So heissen Leute, die sich selbst sehen' (So people who see themselves are called). Ibid., p. 1.

23 For a biographical sketch and brief review of his contribution to visual anthropology especially on understanding the impact of film and photography on traditional tribal peoples, see Harald Prins and John Bishop, 'Edmund Carpenter: Explorations in media & anthropology', *Visual Anthropology Review* 17:2 (2001), pp. 110–40.

24 Edmund Carpenter, 'The tribal terror of awareness', in Paul Hockings, ed., *Principles of Visual Anthropology* (The Hague: Mouton, 1975), pp. 451–61.

25 Ibid.

26 Ibid., p. 481.

27 Carpenter also writes about a mysterious mirror a government patrol discovered hidden in a thatched roof. The patrol was looking for stolen salt – mirrors where not forbidden in the Papuan plateau. And yet, the use of that mirror, carefully wrapped in bark and hidden away remained an unsolved riddle. Carpenter never discovered its purpose or the reason it was concealed and out of sight (ibid.).

28 Ibid., p. 482.

29 Ibid., p. 483.

30 Ibid., p. 190.

31 Ibid., p. 483.

32 Alfred Gell, 'The technology of enchantment and the enchantment of technology', *Anthropology, Art and Aesthetics* 12 (1992), pp. 40–63, 44.

33 Eco, *Semiotics and the Philosophy of Language*, p. 216.

Chapter 3

1   Laura Hurd Clarke and Meridith Griffin, 'Visible and invisible ageing: Beauty work as a response to ageism', *Ageing & Society* 28 (2008), pp. 653–74.

2   Ibid., p. 671.

3   Justine Coupland, 'Dance, ageing and the mirror: Negotiating watchability', *Discourse & Communication* 7:1 (2013), pp. 3–24, 4.

4   Ibid., p. 5.

5   Kathleen Woodward, *Aging and Its Discontents: Freud and Other Fictions* (Bloomington: Indiana University Press, 1991), p. 62.

6   See Chapter 9 for more on this subject.

7   John Berger, *Ways of Seeing* (London: Penguin Books, 1972), p. 8.

8   Elinor Ochs and Lisa Capps, 'Narrating the self', *Annual Review of Anthropology* 25 (1996), pp. 19–43.

9   Julia Twigg, 'Clothing, age and the body: A critical review', *Ageing and Society* 27 (2007), pp. 285–305, 298.

10 Woodward, *Aging and Its Discontents*, p. 62.

11 For more detailed discussion, see Chapter 8.

12 Even though the main target of beauty and fashion industry is women, men are not off the hook. On the contrary, advertising is sending contradictory and confusing messages to men. For a good case of the 'double bind of Masculinity', see Susan Bordo, *The Male Body: A New Look at Men in Public and in Private* (New York: Farrar, Straus and Giroux, 1999).

13 Simon Blackburn, *Mirror, Mirror: The Uses and Abuses of Self-Love* (New Jersey: Princeton University Press, 2014).

14 Ibid., p. 57.

15 Marshall McLuhan, cited in Richard W Pollay, 'The distorted mirror: Reflections on the unintended consequences of advertising', *The Journal of Marketing* 50:2 (1986), pp. 18–36.

16 Ibid., p. 23.

17 Eric Barnouw, *The Sponsor: Notes on a Modern Potentate* (New Jersey: Transaction Publishers, 1978), p. 83.

18 Bernard Stiegler, *Symbolic Misery: The Hyperindustrial Epoch, Volume 1* (Oxford: Polity Press, 2014), p. 3.

19 Vance Packard, cited in ibid., p. 31.

20 Erica Reischer and Kathryn S. Koo, 'The body beautiful: Symbolism and agency in the social world', *Annual Review of Anthropology* 33 (2004), pp. 297–317, 315.

21 Philippe Rochat, *Others in Mind: Social Origins of Self-consciousness* (Cambridge: Cambridge University Press, 2009), pp. 1–2.

22 Ibid., p. 2.

23 Stiegler, *Symbolic Misery*, p. 2.

24 Rochat, *Others in Mind*, p. 3.

25 Clark Baim, Jorge Burmeister, Manuela Maciel, eds., *Psychodrama: Advances in Theory and Practice* (New York: Routledge, 2007), p. 83.

26 J. Miller, *On Reflection* (London: National Gallery Publications/Yale University Press, 1998), p. 13

27 Foucault, M. (1987). 'The ethic of care for the self as a practice of freedom: An interview with Michel Foucault on January 20, 1984 in the final Foucault: Studies on Michel Foucault's last works', *Philosophy & Social Criticism* 12: 2–3 (1987), pp. 112–31.

28 Naomi Wolf, *The Beauty Myth* (London: Random House, 1991), p. 82.

29 Ibid., p. 82.

30 Ibid.

31 Ibid., p. 83.

32 Ibid.

33 Ibid., p. 82.

34 Ibid.

35 Lambros Malafouris and Maria-Danae Koukouti, 'How the body remembers its skills: Memory and material engagement', *Journal of Consciousness Studies* 25:7–8 (2018), pp. 158–80.

36 Maurice Merleau-Ponty, *Phenomenology of Perception*, trans. Collin Smith (London: Routledge & Degan Paul, 1962), p. 82.

37 Ibid., p. 146.

38 Paulo Freire, *Pedagogy of the Oppressed*, trans. Myra Bergman Ramos (London: Penguin Books, 1996).

39 Judith Butler, *Gender Trouble* (Abingdon-on-Thames: Routledge, 2007), p. 132.

40 For an interesting read on the construction of the slender body ideal and body management by capitalist society, see Susan Bordo, *Unbearable Weight: Feminism, Western Culture, and the Body* (Berkely, California: University of California Press, 2004).

41 Enid Schildkrout (2004), 'Inscribing the body', *Annu. Rev. Anthropol.*, 33, pp. 319–44.

42 Abraham Ajibade Adeleke, *Intermediate Yoruba: Language, Culture, Literature, and Religious Beliefs*, part II (Bloomington, Indiana: Trafford Publishing, 2011). Olatunji Ojo, 'Beyond Diversity: Women, Scarification and Yoruba Identity', *History in Africa* 35 (2008), pp. 347–74.

43 Anne Cloudsley, *Women of Omdurman: Life, Love and the Cult of Virginity* (London: Ethnographica, 1983).

Chapter 4

1 Lewis Carroll, *Alice through the Looking-Glass* (London: Walker Books, 2005).

2 Pamela E. Haglund, 'A clear and equal glass: Reflections on the metaphor of the mirror', *Psychoanalytic Psychology* 13:2 (1996), pp. 225–45, 266.

3 Carroll, *Alice through the Looking-Glass*, p. 46.

4 Eduardo Viveiros de Castro, 'Cosmological deixis and Amerindian perspectivism', *The Journal of the Royal Anthropological Institute* 4:3 (1998), pp. 469–88, 469.

5 Ibid., p. 470.

6 Carroll, *Alice through the Looking-Glass*, p. 153.

7 Viveiros de Castro, 'Cosmological deixis and Amerindian perspectivism', pp. 470–1.

8 Ibid.

9 Ibid., p. 272.

10 Philippe Descola, *Beyond Nature and Culture* (Chicago, IL: University of Chicago Press, 2013).

11 Ibid.

12 Sigmund Freud, 'Beyond the pleasure principle', *The Standard Edition of the Complete Psychological Works of Sigmund Freud, Volume XVIII (1920–1922): Beyond the Pleasure Principle, Group Psychology and Other Works* XVIII (1955), pp. 1–64.

13 Jacques Lacan, 'The mirror stage as formative of the function of the I as revealed in psychoanalytic experience', in J.A. Miller, ed. and A. Sheridan, trans., *Ecrits: A Selection* (New York: W. W. Norton, 1977) pp. 97–104.

14 Ibid.

15 Haglund, 'A clear and equal glass', p. 229.

16 Timothy Morton, *Realist Magic: Objects, Ontology, Causality* (London: Open Humanities Press, University of Michigan Library, 2013), p. 17.

Chapter 5

1   Carroll, *Alice through the Looking-Glass.*

2   Jorge Luis Borges, *The Book of Imaginary Beings* (New York: Vintage, 2002).

3   Jorge Luis Borges, *Dreamtigers* trans. Harold Morland (Austin, Texas: University of Texas Press, 1964).

4   Giovanni B. Caputo, 'Strange-face-in-the-mirror illusion', *Perception* 39:7 (2010), pp. 1007–8.

5   Giovanni B. Caputo, 'Archetypal-imaging and mirror-gazing', *Behavioral Sciences* 4:1 (2013), pp. 1–13, 1.

6   J.K. Rowling, *Harry Potter and the Philosopher's Stone* (London: Bloomsbury, 1997).

7   Ibid., p. 152.

8   Ibid., p. 153.

9   Ibid.

10 Ibid.

11 Ibid.

12 Ibid., p. 157.

13 Oscar Wilde, *The Picture of Dorian Gray* (Peterborough, Canada: Broadview Press, 1998).

14 Ibid., p. 77.

15 Ibid., p. 89.

16 Ibid., p. 88.

17 Ibid., p. 77.

18 Ibid., p. 181.

19 Ibid.

20 Ibid.

21 Ibid., p. 183.

22 Jacques Lacan, 'The split between the eye and the gaze', in Alan Sheridan, trans., *The Four Fundamental Concepts of Psychoanalysis* (New York: W. W. Norton, 1978), pp. 67–78 annotation by Phil Lee (Theories of Media, Winter 2003).

23 Giovanni B. Caputo, 'Mask in the mirror: The living mask illusion', *Perception* 40 (2011), pp. 1261–4.

24 Ibid., p. 1261.

25 Ibid., p. 1263.

26 Sylvia Plath, *Collected Poems*, ed. Ted Hughes (London: Faber & Faber, 2002), p. 173.

27 Ibid.

28 Ibid.

Chapter 6

1 Humphrey, 'Inside and outside the mirror', pp. 173–95.

2 Rebecca Empson, 'Separating and containing people and things in Mongolia', eds. Amiria Henare, Martin Holbraad, and Sari Wastell in *Thinking through Things* (London: Routledge, 2007), pp. 139–40.

3 Gregory Delaplace, *L'invention de morts en Mongolie contemporaire: sepultures, fantomes, photographie*, unpublished doctoral thesis in religious anthropology and ethnology (École Pratique des Hautes Études, Paris 2007) cited in Humphrey 'Inside and outside the mirror', p. 178.

4 Humphrey, 'Inside and outside the mirror', p. 178.

5 Empson, 'Separating and containing people and things in Mongolia', cited in Humphrey, 'Inside and outside the mirror', p. 192.

6 For an interesting discussion on how, through Fantasy, modern people try to safely experience the thrill of an enchanted universe, see Alan Jacobs, 'Fantasy and the buffered self', *The New Atlantis* 41 (2014), pp. 3–18.

7 'Shamans' mirrors are circular, range between 6 and 12cm in diameter and are forged from alloys that do not produce clear reflections', note 11 in Katherine Swancutt, 'Representational vs. conjectural divination: Innovating out of nothing in Mongolia', *Journal of the Royal Anthropological Institute* 12 (2006), pp. 331–53.

8 Otgony Pürev, *Mongol böögiin shashin* (Ulaanbaatar: Mongol Ulsyn Shinjleh Uhaaany Akademiin Tüühiin Hüreelen, 1998), in Humphrey, 'Inside and outside the mirror', p. 188.

9   Humphrey, 'Inside and outside the mirror', p. 173.

10   Yuka Kadoi, 'Translating form jing to mira'at/a'ina: Medieval Islamic mirrors
     revisited', *Art in Translation* 5:2 (2013), pp. 251–72.

11   Humphrey, 'Inside and outside the mirror', p. 192.

12   E. Loubo-Lesnitchenko informs us that imported Siberian mirrors are kept in the
     museums of Minusinsk, the University Museum in Tomsk and in the museums
     of Irkutsk, Kranoyarsk and Abakan, while collections of imported mirrors
     exist in the National Historical Museum in Moscow, the National Hermitage in
     Leningrad and the Museum in Helsinki, in E. Loubo-Lesnitchenko, 'Imported
     mirrors in the Minusink Basin', *Artibus Asiae* 35 (1973), pp. 25–61.

13   Walter Heissig, *The Religions of Mongolia* (London: Routledge and Kegan Paul,
     1970), in Humphrey, 'Inside and outside the mirror', p. 177.

14   Ibid., p. 183.

15   Otgony Purev, *Mongolian Shamanism*, trans. G. Purvee, Richard Lawrence and
     Elaine Cheng (Ullanbaatar: Munkhiin Useg, 2005).

16   Humphrey 'Inside and outside the mirror', p. 180.

17   Eduardo Viveiros de Castro, 'Exchanging perspectives: The transformation of
     objects into subjects in Amerindian ontologies', *Common Knowledge* 10 (2004),
     pp. 463–84, 468.

18   Pürev, *Mongol böögiin shashin*, cited in Humphrey, 'Inside and outside the
     mirror', p. 187.

19   Ibid., p. 187 (Humphrey is referencing Purev and Sarangoa in relation to the
     shamans of the Horchin area).

20   Observations concerning the powers of the mirror, the beliefs of the people in
     relation to the mirror and life after death, as well as shamans' practices refer to,
     as Humphrey suggests, the Darhad of Hovsgol in Northwest Mongolia and the
     Horchin of Eastern Mongolia. Also, to the Daurs and the Buryats. Humphrey,
     'Inside and outside the mirror', p. 174.

21   Ibid., p. 189.

22   Japanese Mythology and Folklore, available online at: https://japanesemythology.
     wordpress.com/notes-mirrors-in-history-and-mirror-superstitions/ (Accessed:
     January 2018)

23   For some good examples, see George MacDonald et al., 'Mirrors, portals and
     multiple realities', *Zygon* 23:4 (1998), pp. 39–64.

24   Françoise Frontisi-Ducroux and Jean-Pierre Vernant, *Das l'oeil du miroir* (Paris:
     Éditions Odile Jacob, 1997).

25   Willard McCarty, 'The shape of the mirror: Metaphorical catoptrics in classical
     literature', *Aretusa* 22:2 (1989), pp. 161–5, 174.

26 Ibid., p. 175.

27 Ibid., p. 170.

28 Ibid.

29 Frontisi-Ducroux and Vernant, *Das l'oeil du miroir*, chapter 6.

30 Ibid.

31 Humphrey referring to Olziihutang and Gaadamba, 'Inside and outside the mirror', p. 156.

32 Ibid., pp. 185–6.

33 Ölziihutag and Osor (1989), p. 128 cited in Humphrey, 'Inside and outside the mirror', p. 186.

34 Ibid., p. 175.

35 Swancutt, 'Representational vs. conjectural divination: Innovating out of nothing in Mongolia', *Journal of the Royal Anthropological Institute* 12 (2006), pp. 331–53, 344.

36 Ibid., p. 344.

37 Humphrey, 'Inside and outside the mirror', p. 190.

38 Swancutt, 'Representational vs conjectural divination', p. 331.

39 Ibid., p. 331.

40 Ibid., p. 344.

41 Ibid., p. 350.

42 Old Mongolian riddle, cited in Humphrey, 'Inside and outside the mirror', p. 186.

43 Ibid., p. 190.

44 Raymond Tallis, *The Black Mirror* (London: Atlantic Books, 2016).

45 Ibid., p. 22.

46 Ibid., p. 27.

Chapter 7

1 Beulah Amsterdam, 'Mirror self-image reactions before age two', *Developmental Psychobiology* 5 (1972), pp. 297–305. Gordon Gallup, 'Self-recognition: Research strategies and experimental design', in Sue Taylor Parker, Robert W. Mitchell, and Maria L. Boccia, eds., *Self-awareness in Animals and Humans: Developmental Perspectives* (Cambridge: Cambridge University Press, 1994), pp. 35–50.

2 Rochat and Zahavi, 'The uncanny mirror', p. 212.

3 Malafouris, *How Things Shape the Mind*.

4 Alberto Corsín Jiménez and Chloe Nahum-Claudel, 'The anthropology of traps: Concrete technologies and theoretical interfaces', *Journal of Material Culture* 24:4 (2019), pp. 1–18, 15.

5   Gell, 'Vogel's net', pp. 15–38, 27.

6   Ibid., p. 27.

7   Ibid., p. 26.

8   Ibid.

9   Ibid., p. 27.

10   According to Eco, the mirror is not a sign but it is a prosthesis: 'The magic of
     the mirror lies in the fact that their extensiveness-intrusiveness allows us both
     to have a better look at the world and to look at ourselves as anybody else might;
     it is a unique experience, and mankind knows of no other similar one.' Eco,
     Semiotics and the Philosophy of Language, p. 209.

11   Jean-Paul Sartre, *Nausea*, trans. Robert Baldick (London: Penguin Classics,
     1965), p. 13.

12   Ibid., p. 30.

13   Ibid.

14   Ibid., pp. 30–1.

15   Ibid., p. 31.

16   Ibid.

17   Ibid.

18   Deleuse and Guattari, *A Thousand Plateaus*, p. 200.

19   Sartre, *Nausea*, p. 31.

20   Ibid.

21   Gell, 'Vogel's net', p. 29.

22   Willerslev, 'Not animal, not *not*-animal', pp. 629–52. Willerslev, *Soul hunters*.

23   Philippe Descola, 'Beyond nature and culture: The traffic of souls', *HAU: Journal
     of Ethnographic Theory* 2:1 (2012), pp. 473–500, 474.

24   Willerslev, 'Not animal, not *not*-animal'.

25   Ibid., p. 633.

26   The quote belongs to Waldemar Jochelson (1926) cited in Rane Willerslev, 'Not
     animal, not *not*-animal', p. 634.

27   Ibid., p. 634.

28   Ibid., p. 635.

29   Ibid.

30   Ibid., p. 638.

31   Susan Sontag, *On Photography* (London: Macmillan, 2001), p. 161.

32   Willerslev, 'Not animal, not *not*-animal', p. 635.

33   Ibid., p. 636.

34   Ibid.

35   Ibid., p. 637.

36 Ovid, *Metamorphoses*, trans. & ed. Charles Martin (London: W.W. Norton, 2010).

37 Ibid., p. 75.

38 Ibid., p. 77.

39 Ibid.

40 Ibid., p. 78.

41 Pierre Legendre, Peter Goodrich and Alain Pottage, 'Introduction to the theory of the image: Narcissus and the other in the mirror', *Law Critique* 8:3 (1997), pp. 3–35, 1.

42 Ovid, *Metamorphoses*, p. 78.

43 Ibid.

44 Ibid., p. 79.

45 Ibid., p. 80.

46 Michael Taussig, *Mimesis and Alterity: A Particular History of the Senses* (New York: Routledge, 1993).

47 Ibid.

48 Willerslev, 'Not animal, not *not*-animal', p. 642.

49 Rane Willerslev, 'Spirits as "ready to hand": A phenomenological analysis of Yukaghir spiritual knowledge and dreaming', *Anthropological Theory* 4:4 (2004) pp. 395–418, 410.

50 Ibid.

51 Willerslev, 'Not animal, not *not*-animal', p. 646.

52 Descola, 'Beyond nature and culture: The traffic of souls', p. 474.

53 See Eduardo, 'Cosmological deixis and Amerindian perspectivism', pp. 469–88. Laura Rival, 'The attachment of the soul to the body among the Huaorani of Amazonian Ecuador', *Ethnos* 70:3 (2005), pp. 285–310. Fernando Santos-Granero, 'Beinghood and people-making in native Amazonia: A constructional approach with a perspectival coda', *HAU: Journal of Ethnographic Theory* 2:1 (2012), pp. 181–211.

54 Descola, 'Beyond nature and culture: The traffic of souls', p. 474.

55 Ibid., p. 482.

56 Ibid., p. 493.

57 Sontag, *On Photography*, pp. 178–9.

58 Jorella Andrews, *Showing Off!: A Philosophy of Image* (London: Bloomsbury Publishing, 2014), p. 5.

59 Tim Ingold discusses a symbiotic versus a predatory relationship between man and deer in his article 'On reindeer and men', *Royal Anthropological Institute of Great Britain and Ireland, Man*, New Series, 9:4 (1974), pp. 523–38.

60 Gunter Gebauer and Wulf Christoph, *Mimesis: Culture, Art, Society*, trans. D. Reneau (Berkeley: University of California Press, 1996).

61 Willerslev, 'Not animal, not *not*-animal', p. 644.

Chapter 8

1   Rochat and Zahavi, 'The uncanny mirror'.

2   Ibid., p. 9.

3   Carpenter, *The Tribal Terror of Self-Awareness*, p. 485.

4   Philippe Rochat, 'Five levels of self-awareness as they unfold early in life', *Consciousness and Cognition* 12:4 (2003), pp. 717–31, 720–1.

5   Woodward, *Aging and Its Discontents*, p. 66.

6   Ibid., p. 62.

7   Jean Baudrillard cited in Andrews, *Showing Off!*, p. 4

8   Mirror therapy can be traced as far back as the eighteenth century in South Asian Islamic medicine. Neil Krishan Aggarwal refers to the accounts of Muhammad Akbar Arzani, an influential practitioner of Islamic medicine. In Arzani's records, he writes, we witnessed the beginning (as we so far know) of the mirror therapy concerning the 'Diseases of the Face', a term Arzani used to describe facial paralysis. The symptoms included a weakening of the senses like taste and smell, as well as, the hanging down of bottom eye lid and mouth. The mirror involved in the therapy was described by Arzani as a 'Chinese mirror'(ibid., p. 3). It is a mirror made completely out of metal – melted silver, copper or brass. One was supposed to hold that mirror by cupping their hand against its edge, or by a cord attached to the mirror's back. The therapy involved, among other things, the patient sitting in a dark room, looking continuously in the mirror held in front of her or him. Like the shamanic mirror – a mirror also made completely out of metal – the Chinese mirror could not and was not supposed to offer a precise and clear face reflection. On the contrary, it was used because of its ability to produce optical illusions: the multiplicity of views on its metallic surface conveyed the illusion of straightness, as well as the illusion of movement, on the reflection of the deformed and paralysed face of the patient. What is striking, Aggarwal writes, is Arzani's ability to value the mirror precisely for this ability: the realization, in other words, that a number of deceptive mirror reflections, that is, the reflections of a healthier face, would help the patient to eventually mobilize the paralysed face (p. 3).

    Neil Krishan Aggarwal. 'Mirror therapy for facial paralysis in traditional South Asian Islamic medicine', *Journal of the History of the Neurosciences*, 22:1 (2013), pp. 1–5.

9   Wyona Freysteinson, 'Therapeutic mirror interventions: An integrated review of the literature', *Journal of Holistic Nursing* 27 (2009), pp. 241–52.Sherrie Delinsky and Terence Wilson, 'Mirror exposure for the treatment of body image disturbance', *Internal Journal of Eating Disorders* 39:2 (2006), pp. 108–16.

Trevor Griffen, Eva Naumann, and Tom Hildebrandt, 'Mirror exposure therapy for body image disturbances and eating disorders: A review'. *Clinical Psychology Review* 65 (2018), pp. 163–74.

10 Nili Tabak, Rebecca Bergman, and Rachel Alpert. 'The mirror as a therapeutic tool for patients with dementia', *International Journal of Nursing Practice* 2 (1996), pp. 155–9.

11 J.M. Beis, J.M. Andre, A. Barre, and J. Paysant. 'Mirror images and unilateral special neglect', *Neuropsychologia* 39 (2001), pp. 1444–50.

12 The technique of mirror exposure, as the term suggest, basically involves patients systematically observing themselves in a full-length mirror 'by taking a holistic view as opposed to selectively focusing on body parts that elicit distress, to describe it, to be non-judgmental, and to stay in the present. The goal of this intervention is to help the patient shift from an automatic (and dysfunctional) mind-set to a more controlled one in which she does not dwell on the past, worry about the future, or try to avoid any unpleasant aspect of the experience. The emphasis is on self-acceptance and tolerating negative feelings as they are experienced in the moment. Patients with BN tend to automatically judge their bodies in negative terms. Selective attention on real and perceived imperfections is hypothesized to maintain their dysfunctional concerns about shape and weight. This lack of self-acceptance generates frustration and negative affect, trapping them in a continuing cycle of distress.' See Delinsky and Wilson, 'Mirror exposure for the treatment of body image disturbance', pp. 108–16, 109.

Griffen et.al., 'Mirror exposure therapy for body image disturbances and eating disorders'.

13 V.S. Ramachandran and E.L. Altschuler. 'The use of visual feedback, in particular mirror visual feedback, in restoring brain function', *Brain* 132 (2009), pp. 1693–710. J. Barbin, V. Seetha, J.M. Casillas, J. Paysant, and D. Perennou. 'The effects of mirror therapy on pain and motor control of phantom limb in amputees: A systematic review', *Annals of Physical and Rehabilitation Medicine* 59:4 (2016), pp. 270–5.

L. Herrador Colmenero, J.M. Perez Marmol, C. Martí-García, M.D.L.Á. Querol Zaldivar, R.M. Tapia Haro, A.M. Castro Sánchez, and M.E. Aguilar-Ferrándiz. 'Effectiveness of mirror therapy, motor imagery, and virtual feedback on phantom limb pain following amputation: A systematic review', *Prosthetics and Orthotics International* 42:3 (2018), pp. 288–98.

14 C.Y. Wu, P.C. Huang, Y.T. Chen, K.C. Lin, and H.W. Yang. 'Effects of mirror therapy on motor and sensory recovery in chronic stroke: A randomized controlled trial', *Archives of Physical Medicine and Rehabilitation* 94:6 (2013), pp. 1023–30.

15 A.S. Rothgangel, S.M. Braun, A.J. Beurskens, R.J. Seitz, and D.T. Wade. 'The clinical aspects of mirror therapy in rehabilitation: A systematic review of the literature', *International Journal of Rehabilitation Research* 34:1 (2011), pp. 1–13.

16 Frederik Deconinck, Ana R.P. Smorenburg, Alex Benham, Annick Ledebt, Max G. Feltham and Geert J.P. Savelsbergh, 'Reflections on mirror therapy: A systematic review of the effect of mirror visual feedback on the brain', *Neurorehabilitation and Neural Repair* 29:4 (2015), pp. 349–61. Paul M. Jenkinson, Patrick Haggard, Nicola C. Ferreira and Aikaterini Fotopoulou. 'Body ownership and attention in the mirror: Insights from somatoparaphrenia and the rubber hand illusion', *Neuropsychologia* 51: 8 (2013), pp. 1453–62.

17 Kenji Fukurama, Kenichi Sugawara, Shigeo Tanabe, Junichi Ushiba and Yutaka Tomita, 'Influence of mirror therapy on human motor cortex', *International Journal of Neuroscience* 117:7 (2007), pp. 1039–48.

18 Lone Nikolajsen and Troels Staehelin Jensen, 'Phantom limb pain', *British Journal of Anaesthesia* 87:1 (2001), pp. 107–16 .See also Herta Flor, 'Phantom-limb pain: Characteristics, causes, and treatment', *The Lancet Neurology*, 1:3 (2002), pp. 182–9.

19 See https://www.frontiersin.org/articles/10.3389/fnhum.2017.00483/full (Accessed: May 2019)

20 Vilayanur S. Ramachandran and Diane Rogers-, 'Synaesthesia in phantom limbs induced with mirrors', *Proceedings of the Royal Society of London. Series B: Biological Sciences* 263:1369 (1996), pp. 377–86.

21 Vilayanur S. Ramachandran and Eric Altschuler, 'The use of visual feedback, in particular mirror visual feedback, in restoring brain function', *Brain* 132 (2009), pp. 1693–710.

22 Lorimer Moseley, Alberto Gallace, and Charles Spence, '"Is mirror therapy all it is cracked up to be?" Current evidence and future directions', *Pain* 138 (2008), pp. 7–10.

23 Ramachandran et al., 'The use of visual feedback, in particular mirror visual feedback, in restoring brain function'.

24 Moseley et al., 'Is mirror therapy all it is cracked up to be? Current evidence and future directions', p. 7.

25 Ramachandran et al., 'The use of visual feedback, in particular mirror visual feedback, in restoring brain function'.

26 Shaun Gallagher, 'Philosophical conceptions of the self: Implications for cognitive science', *Trends in Cognitive Sciences* 4:1 (2000), pp. 14–21.

27 Philippe Rochat, 'Self-conscious roots of human normativity', *Phenomenology and the Cognitive Sciences* 14:4 (2015), pp. 741–53.

28 Philippe Rochat, Tanya Broesch and Katherine Jayne, 'Social awareness and early self-recognition', *Consciousness and Cognition* 21:3 (2012), pp. 1491–7.

29   Rochat and Zahavi, 'The uncanny mirror', p. 9.

30   Rochat et al., 'Social awareness and early self-recognition', p. 1496.

31   Rochat and Zahavi, 'The uncanny mirror', p. 9.

32   Ibid.

33   Rochat, *Others in Mind.*

34   Deleuze and Guattari, *A Thousand Plateaus,* p. 174.

35   Ibid., pp. 174–5.

36   Merleau-Ponty, 'Eye and Mind', in J. Edie, ed., *The Primacy of Perception and Other Essays* (Evanston IL: Northwestern University Press, 1964), p. 129.

37   According to neuroscientist Manos Tsakiris, this question is crucial for understanding mirror self-recognition, and more specifically face recognition in the case of humans. Manos Tsakiris, 'Looking for myself: Current multisensory input alters self-face recognition', *PLoS ONE* 3:12 (2008), e4040. https://journals.plos.org/plosone/article?id=10.1371/journal.pone.0004040 (Accessed: January 2016)

38   Diana, 'Reflecting on mirror Self-misrecognition', *Neuropsychoanalysis* 11:2 (2009), p. 214.

39   Karen Postal, 'The mirror sign delusional misidentification symptom', in T. Feinberg and J. Keenan, eds., *The Lost Self: Pathologies of the Brain and Identity* (Oxford: Oxford University Press 2005), pp. 131–46. Nora Breen, Diana Caine and Max Coltheart, 'Mirrored-self misidentification: Two cases of focal onset dementia', *Neurocase* 7 (2001), pp. 239–54. Alberto Villarejo, Verónica Puertas Martin, Teresa Moreno-Ramos, Ana Camacho-Salas, Jesús Porta-Etessam and Félix Bermejo-Pareja, 'Mirrored-self misidentification in a patient without dementia: Evidence for right hemispheric and bifrontal damage', *Neurocase* 17:3 (2011), pp. 276–84.

40   Chandra Sadanandavalli Retnaswami and Thomas Gregor Issac, 'Mirror image agnosia'. *Indian Journal of Psychological Medicine* 36:4 (2014), pp. 400–3. See videos of two patients: https://www.ncbi.nlm.nih.gov/pmc/articles/PMC4201793/#SD1 (Accessed: March 2018) V. S. Ramachandran, E. L. Altschuler, and S. Hillyer, 'Mirror agnosia', *Proceedings of the Royal Society of London. Series B: Biological Sciences* 264:1382 (1997), pp. 645–7.

41   Nora Breen et al., 'Mirrored-self misidentification'. Michael H. Connors and Max Coltheart, 'On the behaviour of senile dementia patients vis-à-vis the mirror: Ajuriaguerra, Strejilevitch and Tissot (1963)', *Neuropsychologia* 49:7 (2011), pp. 1679–92.

42   Lambros Malafouris, 'Thinking as "thinking": Psychology with things', *Current Directions in Psychological Science* 29:1 (2019).

43   Eco, *Semiotics and the Philosophy of Language*, p. 216.

44 Maria Danae Koukouti and Lambros Malafouris, 'Material imagination: An anthropological perspective', in A. Abraham, ed., *The Cambridge Handbook of the Imagination* (Cambridge, England: Cambridge University Press, 2020) pp. 30–46.

45 Foucault, 'The ethic of care for the self as a practice of freedom', p. 131.

Chapter 9

1 Lambros Malafouris, 'Enactive discovery: The aesthetic of material engagement', in R. Manzotti, ed., *Situated Aesthetics: Art beyond the Skin* (Exeter: Imprint Academic, 2011), pp. 123–41.

2 Rochat, 'Five levels of self-awareness as they unfold early in life', pp. 720–1.

3 Terence S. Turner, 'The social skin', *HAU: Journal of Ethnographic Theory* 2:2 [1980] (2012), pp. 486–504. This is a reprint of Terence S. Turner, 'The social skin', in Jeremy Cherfas and Roger Lewin, eds., *Not Work Alone: A Cross-cultural View of Activities Superfluous to Survival* (London: Temple Smith, 1980), 112–40.

4 Gell, '*Vogel's Net*', p. 31.

5 https://www.youtube.com/watch?v=hXQB7RFzoFM (Accessed: January 2018)

6 Bernard Stiegler, 'Suffocated desire, or how the cultural industry destroys the individual: Contribution to a theory of mass consumption', *Parrhesia* 13 (2011), pp. 52–61, 54.

7 Ibid., p. 54.

8 Deleuze and Guattari, *A Thousand Plateaus*.

9 Lambros Malafouris, 'Before and beyond representation: Towards an enactive conception of the Palaeolithic image', in Colin Renfrew and Iain Morley, eds., *Image and Imagination: A Global History of Figurative Representation* (Cambridge: The McDonald Institute for Archaeological Research, University of Cambridge, 2007), pp. 287–300.

10 Hans Belting, *An Anthropology of Images: Picture, Medium, Body* (Princeton NJ: Princeton University Press, 2011), p. 36.

11 John Berger, *Ways of Seeing* (London: Penguin, 2008), p. 9.

References

Adeleke, A.A., *Intermediate Yoruba: Language, Culture, Literature, and Religious Beliefs*, Bloomington, IN: Trafford Publishing, 2011.

Amsterdam, B., 'Mirror self-image reactions before age two', *Developmental Psychobiology* 5 (1972), pp. 297–305

Anderson, M. (ed.), *The Book of the Mirror: An Interdisciplinary Collection Exploring the Cultural History of the Mirror*, Newcastle: Cambridge Scholars Publishing, 2007.

Andrews, J., *Showing Off!: A Philosophy of Image*, London: Bloomsbury Publishing, 2014.

Anzellotti, F., Onofrj, V., Maruotti, V., Ricciardi, L., Franciotti, R., Bonanni, L., Thomas, A., and M. Onofrj, 'Autoscopic phenomena: Case report and review of literature', *Behavioral and Brain Functions* 7:2 (2011), pp. 1–11.

Baim, C., Burmeister, J., and M. Maciel, *Psychodrama: Advances in Theory and Practice*, New York: Taylor and Francis, 2007.

Barad, K., *Meeting the Universe Halfway: Quantum Physics and the Entanglement of Matter and Meaning*, Durham, NC: Duke University Press, 2007.

Barad, K., 'Posthumanist performativity: Toward an understanding of how matter comes to matter', in Stacey Alaimo and Susan Hekman (eds.), *Material Feminisms*, Bloomington, IN: Indiana University Press 2008, pp. 120–56.

Barbin, J., Seetha, V., Casillas, J.M., Paysant, J., and D., Perennou, 'The effects of mirror therapy on pain and motor control of phantom limb in amputees: A systematic review', *Annals of Physical and Rehabilitation Medicine* 59:4 (2016), pp. 270–5.

Barnouw, E., *The Sponsor: Notes on a Modern Potentate* (Vol. 580), New Jersey: Transaction Publishers, 1978.

Barthes, R., *Camera Lucida: Reflections on Photography*, London: Vintage, 1993.

Bateson, G., *Mind and Nature. A Necessary Unity*, New York: Bentam Books, 1979.

Behrend, H., 'Photo magic: Photographs in practices of healing and harming in east Africa', *Journal of Religion in Africa* 33:2 (2003), pp. 129–45.

Belting, H., *An Anthropology of Images: Picture, Medium, Body*, Princeton, NJ: Princeton University Press, 2014.

Beis, J.M., Andre, J.M., Barre, A., and J. Paysant, 'Mirror images and unilateral special neglect', *Neuropsychologia* 39 (2001), pp. 1444–50.

Berger, J., *Ways of Seeing*, London: Penguin UK, 2008.

Bennett, J., *Vibrant Matter: A Political Ecology of Things*, Durham, NC: Duke University Press, 2010.

Bertamini, M., and T.E. Parks, 'On what people know about images on mirrors', *Cognition* 98:1 (2005), pp. 85–104.

Blackburn, S., *Mirror, Mirror: The Uses and Abuses of Self-love*, Woodstock, This should be: Woodstock, Oxfordshire: Princeton University Press, 2014.

Blanke, O., and S., Arzy, 'The out-of-body experience: Disturbed self-processing at the temporo-parietal junction', *The Neuroscientist* 11:1 (2005), pp. 16–24.

Bordo, S., *The Male Body: A New Look at Men in Public and in Private*, New York: Macmillan, 2000.

Bordo, S., *Unbearable Weight: Feminism, Western Culture, and the Body*, Berkely, CA: University of California Press, 2004.

Borges, J.L., *Dreamtigers*, trans. Harold Morland, Austin, TX: University of Texas Press, 1964.

Borges, J.L., *The Book of Imaginary Beings*, New York: Vintage, 2002.

Breen, N., Caine, D., and M. Coltheart, 'Mirrored-self misidentification: Two cases of focal onset dementia', *Neurocase* 7 (2001), pp. 239–54.

Butler, J., *Gender Trouble*, Abingdon-on-Thames: Routledge, 2007

Caine, D., 'Reflecting on mirror self-misrecognition', *Neuropsychoanalysis* 11:2 (2009), pp. 211–26.

Carroll, L., *Alice through the Looking-Glass*, London: Walker Books, 2005.

Carpenter, Edmund, 'The tribal terror of self-awareness', in Paul Hockings (ed.) *Principles of Visual Anthropology*, The Hague: Mouton, 1975, pp. 451–61.

Caputo, G.B., 'Strange-face-in-the-mirror illusion', *Perception* 39:7 (2010), pp. 1007–8.

Caputo, G.B., 'Mask in the mirror: The living mask illusion', *Perception* 40 (2011), pp. 1261–4.

Caputo, G.B., 'Archetypal-imaging and mirror-gazing', *Behavioral Sciences* 4:1 (2013), pp. 1–13.

Chandra, S.R., and T.G. Issac, 'Mirror image agnosia', *Indian Journal of Psychological Medicine* 36:4 (2014), pp. 400–3.

Clarke, L.H., and M. Griffin, 'Visible and invisible ageing: Beauty work as a response to ageism', *Ageing & Society* 28:5 (2008), pp. 653–74.

Connors, M.H., and M. Coltheart, 'On the behaviour of senile dementia patients vis-à-vis the mirror: Ajuriaguerra, Strejilevitch and Tissot (1963)', *Neuropsychologia* 49:7 (2011), pp. 1679–92.

Coole, D., and S., Frost (eds.), *New Materialisms: Ontology, Agency, and Politics*, Durham, NC: Duke University Press, 2010.

Corsín Jiménez, A., and C. Nahum-Claudel, 'The anthropology of traps: Concrete technologies and theoretical interfaces', *Journal of Material Culture* 24:4 (2019), pp. 1–18.

Coupland, J., 'Dance, ageing and the mirror: Negotiating watchability', *Discourse & Communication* 7:1 (2013), pp. 3–24.

Cloudsley, A., *Women of Omdurman: Life, Love and the Cult of Virginity*, London: Ethnographica, 1983.

Derrida, J., 'Le cinéma et ses fantômes', *Cahiers du cinéma* 556 (2001), pp. 74–85.

Deleuze, G., and F., Guattari, *Rhizôme, Introduction*, Paris: Editions de Minuit, 1976.

Deleuze, G., and F., Guattari, *A Thousand Plateaus: Capitalism and Schizophrenia*, Bloomsbury Publishing, 1988.

Descola, P., 'Beyond nature and culture: The traffic of souls', *HAU: Journal of Ethnographic Theory* 2:1 (2012), pp. 473–500.

Descola, P., *Beyond Nature and Culture*, Chicago, IL: University of Chicago Press, 2013.

Deconinck, F.J., Smorenburg, A.R., Benham, A., Ledebt, A., Feltham, M.G., and G.J. Savelsbergh, 'Reflections on mirror therapy: A systematic review of the effect of mirror visual feedback on the brain', *Neurorehabilitation and Neural Repair* 29:4 (2015), pp. 349–61.

Delinsky, S.S., and G.T. Wilson, 'Mirror exposure for the treatment of body image disturbance', *Internal Journal of Eating Disorders* 39:2 (2006), pp. 108–16.

Diefenbach, S., and L. Christoforakos, 'The selfie paradox: Nobody seems to like them yet everyone has reasons to take them. An exploration of psychological functions of selfies in self-presentation', *Frontiers in Psychology* 8 (2017), p. 7.

Eco, U., *Semiotics and the Philosophy of Language*, Bloomington: Indiana University Press, 1984.

Edkins, J., 'Dismantling the face: Landscape for another politics?', *Environment and Planning D: Society and Space* 31:3 (2013), pp. 538–53.

Empson, R., 'Separating and containing people and things in Mongolia', in Amiria Henare, Martin Holbraad, and Sari Wastell (eds.,), *Thinking through Things*, London: Routledge 2007, pp. 123–50.

Flor, H., 'Phantom-limb pain: Characteristics, causes, and treatment', *The Lancet Neurology*, 1:3 (2002), pp. 182–9.

Frontisi-Ducroux, F., and J.P. Vernant, *Dans l'oeil du miroir*. Paris: Odile Jacob, 1997.

Foucault, M., *Discipline and Punish: The Birth of the Prison*, New York: Vintage, 1977.

Freud, S., 'Beyond the pleasure principle', in *The Standard Edition of the Complete Psychological Works of Sigmund Freud, Volume XVIII (1920–1922): Beyond the Pleasure Principle, Group Psychology and Other Works*, xviii, New York: Group Psychology and Other Works, 1955, pp. 1–64.

Freire, P., *Pedagogy of the Oppressed*, trans. Myra Bergman Ramos, London: Penguin Books, 1996.

Freysteinson, W.M., 'Therapeutic mirror interventions: An integrated review of the literature', *Journal of Holistic Nursing*, 27 (2009), pp. 241–52.

Foucault, M., 'The ethic of care for the self as a practice of freedom: An interview with Michel Foucault on January 20, 1984 in the final Foucault: Studies on Michel Foucault's last works', *Philosophy & Social Criticism* 12:2–3 (1987), pp. 112–31.

Fukumura, K., Sugawara, K., Tanabe, S., Ushiba, J., and Y. Tomita, 'Influence of mirror therapy on human motor cortex', *International Journal of Neuroscience*, 117:7 (2007), pp. 1039–48.

Gandy, O., *The Panoptic Sort: Critical Studies in Communication and in the Cultural Industries*, Westvie: Boulder, 1993.

Gallagher, S., 'Philosophical conceptions of the self: Implications for cognitive science', *Trends in Cognitive Sciences* 4:1 (2000), pp.14–21.

Gallup, G.G., 'Self-recognition: Research strategies and experimental design', in S.T. Parker, R.W. Mitchell and M.L. Boccia (eds.), *Self-awareness in Animals and Humans: Developmental Perspectives*, Cambridge: Cambridge University Press, 1994, pp. 35–50.

Gebauer, G., and C. Wulf, *Mimesis: Culture Art Society*, Berkeley, California: University of California Press, 1995.

Gell, A., 'The technology of enchantment and the enchantment of technology', in Jeremy Coote and Anthony Shelton (eds.), *Anthropology, Art and Aesthetics*, Oxford: Clarendon Press, 1992, pp.40–63.

Gell, A., 'Vogel's Net: Traps as artworks and artworks as traps', *Journal of Material Culture* 1:1 (1996), pp. 15–38.

Gordon, G. Gallup, James R. Anderson, and S.M. Platek, 'Self recognition', in Shaun Gallagher (ed.), *The Oxford Handbook of the Self*, Oxford: Oxford University Press, 2011, pp. 80–111.

Gombrich, E.H., *Art and Illusion*, Oxford: Phaidon Press, 1960.

Griffen, T.C., E. Naumann, and T. Hildebrandt, 'Mirror exposure therapy for body image disturbances and eating disorders: A review', *Clinical Psychology Review* 65 (2018), pp. 163–74.

Grüsser, O.J., and T. Landis, 'The splitting of "I" and "me": Heautoscopy and related phenomena', eds. Grüsser O.J., Landis T in *Visual Agnosias and Other Disturbances of Visual Perception and Cognition*, Amsterdam: Macmillan (1991), pp. 297–303.

Haglund, P.E., 'A clear and equal glass: Reflections on the metaphor of the mirror', *Psychoanalytic Psychology* 13:2 (1996), pp. 225–45.

Herrador Colmenero, L., Perez Marmol, J.M., Martí-García, C., Querol Zaldivar, M.D.L.Á., Tapia Haro, R.M., Castro Sánchez, A.M., and M.E. Aguilar-Ferrándiz, 'Effectiveness of mirror therapy, motor imagery, and virtual feedback on phantom limb pain following amputation: A systematic review', *Prosthetics and Orthotics International* 42:3 (2018), pp. 288–98.

Holbraad, M., and M.A. Pedersen, *The Ontological Turn: An Anthropological Exposition*, Cambridge: Cambridge University Press, 2016.

Humphrey, C., 'Inside and outside the mirror: Mongolian Shamans' mirrors as instruments of perspectivism', *Inner Asia* 9 (2007), pp. 173–95.

Ingold, T., 'On reindeer and men', *Royal Anthropological Institute of Great Britain and Ireland, Man* 9:4 (1974), pp. 523–38.

Ingold, T., *Being Alive: Essays on Movement, Knowledge and Description*, London: Routledge, Taylor & Francis, 2011.

Ingold T., *The Life of Lines*, Abingdon-on-Thames: Routledge, 2015.

Ingold, T., and G. Palsson (eds.), *Biosocial Becomings: Integrating Social and Biological Anthropology*, Cambridge: Cambridge University Press, 2013.

Jacobs, A., 'Fantasy and the buffered self', *The New Atlantis* 41 (2014), pp. 3–18.

Jenkinson, P.M., Haggard, P., Ferreira, N.C., and Fotopoulou, A., 'Body ownership and attention in the mirror: Insights from somatoparaphrenia and the rubber hand illusion' *Neuropsychologia* 51:8 (2013), pp. 1453–62.

Kadoi, Y., 'Translating form jing to mira'at/a'ina: Medieval Islamic Mirrors Revisited', *Art in Translation* 5:2 (2013), pp. 251–72.

Koukouti, M.D., and L. Malafouris, 'Material imagination: An anthropological perspective', in Abraham A. (ed.), *The Cambridge Handbook of the Imagination*, Cambridge: Cambridge University Press, 2020. pp. 30–46.

Krishan, A.N., 'Mirror therapy for facial paralysis in traditional South Asian Islamic medicine', *Journal of the History of the Neurosciences* 22:1 (2013), pp.1–5.

Lacan, J., 'The mirror stage as formative of the function of the I as revealed in psychoanalytic experience', in J.A. Miller (ed.) and A. Sheridan (trans.), *Ecrits: A selection*, New York: W. W. Norton, 1977, pp. 97–104.

Lacan, J., 'The split between the eye and the gaze', trans. Alan Sheridan, in *The Four Fundamental Concepts of Psychoanalysis*, New York: W. W. Norton, 1978, pp. 67–78.

Latour B., *Reassembling the Social: An Introduction to Actor-Network-Theory*, Oxford: Oxford University Press, 2007.

Legendre, P., Goodrich, P., and A. Pottage, 'Introduction to the theory of the image: Narcissus and the other in the mirror', *Law and Critique* 8:1 (1997), pp. 3–35.

Lévi-Strauss, C., 'Guerre et commerce chez les Indiens d'Amérique du Sud', *Renaissance* 1 (1943), pp. 122–39.

MacDonald G.F., Cove J.L., Laughlin C.D., and J. McManus, 'Mirrors, portals, and multiple realities', *Zygon*° 24:1 (1989), pp. 39–64.

Malafouris, L., 'Before and beyond representation: Towards an enactive conception of the Palaeolithic image', in C. Renfrew and I. Morley (eds.), *Image and Imagination: A Global History of Figurative Representation*, Cambridge: The McDonald Institute, 2007, pp. 287–300.

Malafouris, L., 'Beads for a plastic mind: The "Blind Man's Stick" (BMS) hypothesis and the active nature of material culture', *Cambridge Archaeological Journal* 18 (2008), pp. 401–14.

Malafouris, L., 'Metaplasticity and the human becoming: Principles of neuroarchaeology', *Journal of Anthropological Sciences* 88 (2010), pp. 49–72.

Malafouris, L., 'Enactive discovery: The aesthetic of material engagement', in R. Manzotti (ed.), *Situated Aesthetics: Art beyond the Skin*, Exeter: Imprint Academic, 2011, pp. 123–41.

Malafouris, L., 'Learning to see: Enactive discovery and the prehistory of pictorial skill', in Klaus Sachs-Hombach and Jorg R. J. Schirra (eds.), *Origins of Pictures: Anthropological Discourses in Picture Science*, Koln: Halem Verlag, 2012, pp. 72–88.

Malafouris, L., *How Things Shape the Mind: A Theory of Material Engagement*, Cambridge, MA: MIT Press, 2013.

Malafouris, L., 'Metaplasticity and the primacy of material engagement', *Time and Mind* 8:4 (2015), pp. 351–71.

Malafouris, L., 'On human becoming and incompleteness: A material engagement approach to the study of embodiment in evolution and culture', in Gregor Etzelmüller and Christian Tewes (eds.), *Embodiment in Evolution and Culture*, Tübingen Mohr Siebeck, 2016, pp. 289–306.

Malafouris, L., and C. Renfrew, 'The cognitive life of things: Archaeology, material engagement and the extended mind', in Lambros Malafouris and Colin Renfrew (eds.), *The Cognitive Life of Things: Recasting the Boundaries of the Mind*, Cambridge: McDonald Institute Monographs, 2010, pp. 1–12.

Malafouris, L., and M.D. Koukouti, 'How the body remembers its skills: Memory and material engagement', *Journal of Consciousness Studies* 25:7-8 (2018), pp. 158–80.

Marwick, A.E., 'Instafame: Luxury selfies in the attention economy', *Public Culture* 27:175 (2015), pp. 137–60.

Mavor, C., 'Collecting Loss', *Cultural Studies* 11:1 (1997), pp. 111–37.

McCarty, W., 'The shape of the mirror: Metaphorical catoptrics in classical literature', *Aretusa* 22:2 (1989), pp. 161–5.

Merleau-Ponty, M., *Phenomenology of Perception*, trans. Collin Smith, London: Routledge & Degan Paul, 1962.

Merleau-Ponty, M., 'Eye and mind', in J. Edie (ed.), *The Primacy of Perception and Other Essays*, Evanston, IL: Northwestern University Press, 1964 pp. 159–192.

Mitchell, W.J.T., 'What is an image?' *New Literary History* 15 (1984), pp. 503–37.

Mitchell, W.J.T., *What Do Pictures Want?: The Lives and Loves of Images*. Chicago, IL: University of Chicago Press, 2005.

Milivojević, T., and I. Ercegovac, '# Selfie or virtual mirror to new Narcissus', *Medijska istraživanja: znanstveno-stručni časopis za novinarstvo i medije* 20:2 (2014), pp. 293–312.

Morton, T., *Realist Magic: Objects, Ontology, Causality*, London: Open Humanities Press, University of Michigan Library, 2013.

Moseley A.G., Gallace, A., and C. Spence, 'Is mirror therapy all it is cracked up to be?' Current evidence and future directions', *Pain* 138 (2008), pp. 7–10.

Nadar, F., Tournachon, G.F., and T., Repensek, 'My life as a photographer', *October* 5 (1978), pp. 7–28.

Nikolajsen, L., and T.S. Jensen, 'Phantom limb pain', *British Journal of Anaesthesia* 87:1 (2001), pp. 107–16.

Ochs, E., and L. Capps, 'Narrating the self', *Annual Review of Anthropology* 25:1 (1996), pp. 19–43.

Ojo, O., 'Beyond diversity: Women, scarification, and Yoruba identity', *History in Africa* 35 (2008), pp. 347–74.

Ovid, *Metamorphoses*, trans, & ed. Charles Martin, London: W.W. Norton, 2010.

Pendergrast, M., *Mirror, Mirror: A History of the Human Love Affair with Reflection*, New York: Basic Books, 2009.

Plath, S., *Collected Poems*, ed. Ted Hughes, London: Faber & Faber, 2002.

Pollay, R.W., 'The distorted mirror: Reflections on the unintended consequences of advertising', *Journal of Marketing* 50:2 (1986), pp. 18–36.

Postal, K.S., 'The mirror sign delusional misidentification symptom', in T. Feinberg and J. Keenan (eds.), *The Lost Self: Pathologies of the Brain and Identity*, 2005 pp. 131–46.

Prins, H.E., and J. Bishop, 'Edmund carpenter: Explorations in media & anthropology', *Visual Anthropology Review* 17:2 (2001), pp. 110–40.

Purev, O., *Mongolian Shamanism*, trans. G. Purvee, Richard Lawrence, and Elaine Cheng, Ullanbaatar: Munkhiin Useg, 2005.

Ramachandran, V.S., and D. Rogers-Ramachandran, 'Synaesthesia in phantom limbs induced with mirrors', *Proceedings of the Royal Society of London. Series B: Biological Sciences* 263:1369 (1996), pp. 377–86.

Ramachandran V.S., and E.L. Altschuler, 'The use of visual feedback, in particular mirror visual feedback, in restoring brain function', *Brain* 132 (2009), pp. 1693–710.

Ramachandran, V.S., E.L. Altschuler, and S. Hillyer., 'Mirror agnosia', *Proceedings of the Royal Society of London. Series B: Biological Sciences* 264:1382 (1997), pp. 645–7.

Rietveld, E., and J. Kiverstein, 'A rich landscape of affordances', *Ecological Psychology* 26:4 (2014), pp. 325–52.

Rival, L., 'The attachment of the soul to the body among the Huaorani of Amazonian Ecuador', *Ethnos* 70:3 (2005), pp. 285–310.

Rochat, P., 'Origin of self-concept', in G. Bremner and A. Foge (eds.), *Blackwell Handbook of Infant Development*, Oxford: Blackwell, 2001, pp. 191–212.

Rochat, P., 'Five levels of self-awareness as they unfold early in life', *Consciousness and Cognition* 12:4 (2003), pp. 717–31.

Rochat, P., *Others in Mind: Social Origins of Self-consciousness*, Cambridge: Cambridge University Press, 2009.

Rochat, P., 'Self-conscious roots of human normativity' *Phenomenology and the Cognitive Sciences* 14:4 (2015), pp. 741–53.

Rochat, P., and D. Zahavi, 'The uncanny mirror: A re-framing of mirror self-experience', *Consciousness and Cognition* 20:2 (2011), pp. 204–13.

Rochat, P., Broesch, T., and K., Jayne, 'Social awareness and early self-recognition', *Consciousness and Cognition* 21:3 (2012), pp. 1491–7.

Rothgangel, A.S., Braun, S.M., Beurskens, A.J., Seitz, R.J., and D.T. Wade, 'The clinical aspects of mirror therapy in rehabilitation: A systematic review of the literature', *International Journal of Rehabilitation Research* 34:1 (2011), pp. 1–13.

Rowling, J.K., *Harry Potter and the Philosopher's Stone*, London: Bloomsbury, 1997.

Saltz, J., 'Art at arm's length: A history of the selfie', *New York Magazine* 47:2 (2014), pp. 71–5.

Santos-Granero, F., 'Beinghood and people-making in native Amazonia: A constructional approach with a perspectival coda', *HAU: Journal of Ethnographic Theory* 2:1 (2012), pp. 181–211.

Sartre, Jean-Paul., *Nausea*, trans. Robert Baldick, London: Penguin Classiscs, 1965.

Sennett, R., *The Craftsman*, New Haven: Yale University Press, 2008.

Schildkrout, E., 'Inscribing the body', *Annu. Rev. Anthropol.* 33 (2004), pp. 319–44.

Schwartz, L.G., 'Cinema and the meaning of "life"', *Discourse* 28:2 (2006), pp. 7–27.

Shin, Y., Minji K., Chaerin I., and Sang Chul Chong, 'Selfie and self: The effect of selfies on self-esteem and social sensitivity', *Personality and Individual Differences* 111 (2017), pp. 139–45.

Sontag, S., *On Photography*, London: Macmillan, 2001.

Stiegler, B., 'Suffocated desire, or how the cultural industry destroys the individual: Contribution to a theory of mass consumption', *Parrhesia* 13 (2011), pp. 52–61.

Stiegler, B., *Symbolic Misery Volume 1: The Hyperindustrial Epoch*, Cambridge: Polity, 2014.

Sung, Y., Jung-Ah Lee, Eunice Kim, and Sejung Marina Choi, 'Why we post selfies: Understanding motivations for posting pictures of oneself', *Personality and Individual Differences* 97 (2016), pp. 260–5.

Swancutt K., 'Representational vs. conjectural divination: Innovating out of nothing in Mongolia', *Journal of the Royal Anthropological Institute* 12 (2006), 331–53.

Tabak, N., Bergman, R., and R., Alpert, 'The mirror as a therapeutic tool for patients with dementia', *International Journal of Nursing Practice* 2 (1996), pp. 155–9.

Tallis, R., *The Black Mirror*, London: Atlantic Books, 2016.

Taussig, M., *Mimesis and Alterity: A Particular History of the Senses*, New York: Routledge, 1993.

Tsakiris, M., 'Looking for myself: Current multisensory input alters self-face recognition', *PLoS ONE* 3:12 (2008), e4040.

Twigg, J., 'Clothing, age and the body: A critical review', *Ageing & Society* 27:2 (2007), pp. 285–305.

Turchi, P., *Maps of the Imagination: The Writer as Cartographer*, San Antonio, TX: Trinity University Press, 2004.

Turner, T.S., 'The social skin', *HAU: Journal of Ethnographic Theory* 2:2 [1980] (2012), pp. 486–504.

Villarejo, A., Martin, V.P., Moreno-Ramos, T., Camacho-Salas, A., Porta-Etessam, J., and F., Bermejo-Pareja, 'Mirrored-self misidentification in a patient without dementia: Evidence for right hemispheric and bifrontal damage', *Neurocase* 17:3 (2011), pp. 276–84.

Viveiros de Castro, E., 'Cosmological deixis and Amerindian perspectivism', *Journal of the Royal Anthropological Institute* 4:3 (1998), pp. 469–88.

Viveiros de Castro, E., Exchanging perspectives: the Transformation of objects into subjects in Amerindian ontologies', *Common Knowledge* 10 (2004), pp. 463–84.

Wilde, O., *The Picture of Dorian Gray*, Peterborough, Canada: Broadview Press, 1998.

Willerslev, R., 'Not animal, not not-animal: Hunting, imitation, and empathetic knowledge among the Siberian Yukaghirs' *Journal of the Royal Anthropological Institute* 10 (2004), pp. 629–52.

Willerslev, R., 'Spirits as "ready to hand": A phenomenological analysis of Yukaghir spiritual knowledge and dreaming', *Antropological Theory* 4:4 (2004) pp. 395–418.

Willerslev, R., *Soul Hunters: Hunting, Animism, and Personhood among the Siberian Yukaghirs*, London: University of California Press, 2007.

Wolf, N., *The Beauty Myth: How Images of Beauty Are Used against Women*. London: Random House, 1991.

Woodward K.M., *Aging and Its Discontents: Freud and Other Fictions*, Bloomington: Indiana University Press, 1991.

Wu, C.Y., Huang, P.C., Chen, Y.T., Lin, K.C., and H.W. Yang, 'Effects of mirror therapy on motor and sensory recovery in chronic stroke: A randomized controlled trial', *Archives of Physical Medicine and Rehabilitation* 94:6 (2013), pp. 1023–30.

Index

www.ingramcontent.com/pod-product-compliance
Lightning Source LLC
Chambersburg PA
CBHW071418290326
41932CB00046B/2237